TOWARD GENDER EQUITY
IN THE CLASSROOM

SUNY Series, Teacher Preparation
and Development
Alan R. Tom, Editor

TOWARD GENDER EQUITY IN THE CLASSROOM

Everyday Teachers' Beliefs and Practices

JANICE STREITMATTER

State University
of New York
Press

Published by
State University of New York Press, Albany

Production by Susan Geraghty
Marketing by Fran Keneston

Printed in the United States of America

For information, address State University of New York Press,
State University Plaza, Albany, NY 12246

Library of Congress Cataloging-in-Publication Data

Streitmatter, Janice, 1952–
     Toward gender equity in the classroom : everyday teachers' beliefs
and practices / Janice Streitmatter.
          p.   cm. — (SUNY series, teacher preparation and development)
     Includes bibliographical references (p.) and index.
     ISBN 0-7914-1803-0 — ISBN 0-7914-1804-9 (pbk.)
     1. Sexism in education—United States. 2. Educational
equalization—United States. 3. Teaching. I. Title. II. Series:
SUNY series in teacher preparation and development.
LC212.2.S77   1994
370.19'345—dc20   93-20334
                                                               CIP

10 9 8 7 6 5 4 3 2

CONTENTS

ACKNOWLEDGMENTS

This book came about through the support and collaboration of a number of people. Special thanks to Alan Tom, who resisted nagging but urged me on and critiqued and supported my efforts throughout. Thanks, too, to Priscilla Ross, who consistently provided gentle and constructive support. Julie Powers, Kay Stritzel, Melanie Cook, Sam Turner, Frank Klajda, Barb Piaseki, Barry Roth, And Paula Pluta provided their collaborative efforts, their thoughtful reflection, and their hospitality without hesitation.

My husband, mother, and late father all were interested and participated in their own ways. Lastly, to Courtney: This is for you and your generation.

PREFACE

This book grew out of an interest in gender issues in schools that dates back to my high-school years. I spent a particularly nasty year with a trigonometry teacher who enjoyed telling the few girls in the class that they were "naturally" unqualified to be taking upper-level mathematics. While I have harbored a bit of residual anger toward "Mr. F." all these years, my interest in gender issues was fully renewed when my daughter, then in first grade, began to bring up her own gender-related concerns. Early in October she complained, "The teacher always seems to call on the boys." Shortly before winter vacation she asked, "Why don't we ever read stories with girls as the main character?" One evening in the early spring she explained that she could not wear a skirt or dress to school the following day because it was "flip-up day." When I looked puzzled, she informed me that "flip-up day is any day that the boys say they will flip-up girls' skirts. Last time I told the boys to stop, but they wouldn't, so I guess the only thing I can do is to wear pants." Courtney reminded me that important issues of gender differentiation and bias remain in classrooms today.

The issue of gender equity in teaching is still largely ignored in classrooms of practicing teachers. The passage of Title IX approximately twenty years ago has gone a long way to ensure that overt gender discrimination, or the limitation of access to educational opportunities, no longer takes place. However, a substantial body of research points unerringly to the conclusion that gender bias, built on unconscious acceptance of gender stereotypes and gender role expectations, continues to be present on a large scale in classrooms.

Because I believe gender equity is a real issue, not simply a topic that is currently "politically correct", and is deeply connected to a teacher's ability to empower all students during their time in the classroom, learning about gender equity ought to be an essential component of a teacher's initial or continuing training. To that end, this book is for initial teacher-preparation students, practicing teachers enhancing the skills and understanding of their craft, or other gender-equity novices who wish to learn more about gender equity in teaching.

Various aspects and considerations of gender equity in teaching are presented through conversations with and observations of eight teachers as well as through a discussion of the pertinent research from the literature. The work which provided the data presented throughout the book examined the various points of view and methods of the eight teachers, who indicated a philosophical as well as a practice-related commitment to gender equity. These teachers not only speak of gender equity as an issue that is important to them on a societal scale, but they also believe that they actively work to implement gender equity into their teaching on a daily basis. The extent to which the teachers incorporate various methods, espouse a particular perspective of gender equity, or impose discipline in a way that is free of gender bias varies greatly. The reader is provided with examples of beliefs about the issues, many methods and techniques adopted by the teachers, and illustrations of gender equity in teaching in classes of various ages of students and content areas.

The analysis of the teachers' classroom practice is based on the time I spent with the teachers, both in discussions and in watching them teach. The discussions focused on the teachers' beliefs about the nature of gender bias and gender equity in the larger society as well as in schools, and on their gender-equity related actions in their classrooms. These discussions included questions from me about the teachers' personal experiences as children and adults, their beliefs about their role as a catalyst for change in the gender-related attitudes of their students and colleagues, and their ideas about the most appropriate methods to counter gender bias.

I spent 15–20 hours in each of the teacher's classrooms over a period of five months. The middle- and high-school teachers were observed during the same class periods; I attempted to observe the elementary teachers at various times throughout the teaching day. The preschool teacher was observed for the entire time she met with her students, 9 A.M. until noon. My observations of the teachers in their classrooms were directed by categories based on the body of research that delineates the various aspects of gender bias and gender equity in schools. These categories in general deal with teacher behavior with students, student behavior with the teacher, and students' behavior among themselves. Specifically, the categories involve students' participation by gender in the lesson or portion of the curriculum, the teacher's methods of language choice and classroom organization, and the teacher's interactions with students by gender (See Appendix A for interview and observation forms).

Each chapter examines various aspects of gender bias and gender equity. Chapter 1 introduces the concept of gender equity as a broader societal issue as well as one that pertains to schooling. Also introduced are the conceptual frameworks of *equality* and *equitable*, the philosophical bases upon which the teachers integrate gender equity into their teaching.

Chapter 2 briefly discusses the history of the development of gender roles and looks at the influence of gender role stratification on males and females in earlier and current schools.

Chapters 3, 4, and 5 combine the information from my discussions with the teachers and my time spent observing their classes and from research pertinent to the discussion of gender equity in teaching. Chapter 3 examines school curriculum and instructional materials as gender equity issues. The research presented describes the various forms of gender bias in females' and males' participation in school curricula and the forms of gender bias found in instructional materials. Descriptions of the curricula and instructional materials used by five of the teachers are provided to illustrate various perspectives and methods used to enhance gender equity.

Chapter 4 is a discussion of two specific methods employed by several of the teachers in their pursuit of gender equity in their classrooms. The teachers' choice of language intended to counter gender stereotypes and bias, and the organizational structure of the classrooms of four of the teachers are described as examples of gender-equitable practice. Also presented is research that analyzes how gender bias is exhibited in teachers' language and in some organizational structures of classrooms.

Chapter 5 examines the pertinent research as well as the practices of five of the teachers that relate to gender equity and teacher-initiated interactions with students. The quality and quantity of teacher-initiated interactions by gender in classrooms also are discussed.

Chapter 6 provides the reader with a basis for developing a personal analysis of the best means to interpret and understand gender equity teaching practice in classrooms. In this chapter the frameworks of *equality* and *equitable* are reconsidered and three teachers' classroom methods are reviewed. Finally, several additional challenges in integrating gender equity into classroom practice are provided and the issue of gender bias in classroom discipline practice is discussed. Also examined are the teachers' perceptions of support and resistance in their efforts to incorporate gender equity in their teaching, and the teachers offer suggestions to "gender-equity novices."

CHAPTER 1

Introducing Gender Equity

This chapter provides some basic terms and concepts about gender bias and gender equity, particularly as they relate to schooling in the United States. Gender discrimination and gender bias are discussed in the first part of the chapter, as are the two conceptual frameworks of equal inputs and equitable outcomes, which provide an understanding of the purpose and implementation of gender equity in classrooms. The second part of the chapter introduces eight teachers whose classrooms illustrate a variety of perspectives about gender equity and methods of implementation via the teachers' attempts to make gender equity an integral part of their teaching.

As part of the Education Amendment Act, Title IX was passed into law in 1972 at a time when various groups demanded greater participation and recognition for themselves in American society and for their children in the schools and when substantial numbers of women and men recognized gender discrimination and bias as equal rights issues. The intent of Title IX is expressed in its preamble:

> No person in the United States shall, on the basis of sex be excluded from participation in, be denied the benefits of, or be subjected to discrimination under any education program or activity receiving federal financial assistance (National Advisory Council on Women's Educational Progress, 1981).

Because Title IX has been in effect for approximately twenty years, it would be logical for prospective and practicing teachers to assume that Title IX has done its job; that gender inequities are a thing of the past. However, as discussed in the *AAUW Report: How Schools Shortchange Girls* (1992), apathy as well as ignorance about gender discrimination persist. For example, research by Schmuck and Schmuck (AAUW Report, 1992) illustrates that school administrators, in this case those in rural schools, considered gender discrimination concerns to be less than pressing issues. A majority of administrators interviewed expressed attitudes about gender equity in schools that include "'stupid and frivolous' to 'worry about equal opportunities for boys and girls' to 'acknowledgement that their districts complied with the letter of the law but did not go beyond concerns of equal access'" (AAUW Report, 1992). This and other current research (e.g., AAUW Report, 1992; Sadker, Sadker, & Klein 1991) indicate clearly that gender discrimination in schools, denial of access and participation—continues to be a problem. However, because gender discrimination tends to be demonstrated in overt denial of opportunity based on gender, it often is fairly obvious and can be addressed via the enforcement of Title IX.

Less obvious and perhaps more pervasive than gender discrimination is the practice of gender bias. Bias is more subtle than discrimination and therefore more difficult to identify. Gender bias may be defined as the underlying network of assumptions and beliefs held by a person that males and females differ in systematic ways other than physically, that is, in talents, behaviors, or interests (*New Pioneers,* 1975). These beliefs lead the person to make assumptions about others strictly based on gender. For example, a teacher who believes, however unconsciously, that if a child is of a particular gender she or he is likely to do, think, or feel a particular way, these beliefs almost certainly will limit the opportunities of many of the learners in the class.

While not all teachers practice in gender-biased ways, many do. They do so not because they set out to differentiate among their students based on gender but because they do not acknowledge gender equity as an issue in the classroom. By not reflecting upon their own teaching as it may be affected by gender stereotypes and bias, these teachers tend to perpetuate the problem.

There are numerous indicators within our schools and society that point to the conclusion that we as teachers continue to practice gender bias in our classrooms. Among those practices that can be seen as gender-biased are: the extent to which we continue to find occurrences, such as one gender being substantially over- or under-represented in a curriculum offering; teacher expectations related to or affected by student gender; or classroom practices such as teaching methods or discipline that disproportionately affect one gender of student.

GENESIS OF GENDER BIAS

In discussing gender bias with preservice and inservice teachers and other groups of people over the years, a frequent question is: As a society, how have we come to consider females and males so differently? The answer is complex, and the two principal explanations—innate and socialization differences—are only very briefly addressed here. I have included the information about these two perspectives not to attempt to answer the question definitively but rather to remind the reader that considerable research and several theories exist that seek to explain gender differences in many aspects of life.

Innate Differences

Belief in theories about different innate characteristics of females and males may help perpetuate unconscious assumptions that are behind gender-biased practices. If one holds the assumption that important thinking and behavioral pattern differences exist between the genders and these differences are caused by genetic or hormonal factors, one is quite likely to substitute gender stereotype for consideration of the individual learner. Specifically, if teachers believe that boys and girls have different innately determined ways of thinking and learning, they may develop gender-differentiated teaching practices.

One dominant theory of innate gender differences is that females think differently than males. Richmond-Abbott (1983) and later Sadker, Sadker, and Klein (1991) summarized the latest research that has examined the several theories proposing a relationship between sex-linked genes and hormones, and specific abilities and intelligence. Briefly stated, studies that have examined the possible relationship between male hormones and specific abilities often associated with male learners (e.g., spacial ability) have found no evidence to support such a relationship.

Another theory that seeks to support the belief that males and females innately think differently suggests that gender-specific hormones help shape abilities through brain development. Much of the research on hormones begins with the assumption that the left and right hemispheres of the brain each process information in a different manner. A good deal of this type of research is currently being conducted, much of it on laboratory animals. At best, the results of the research are inconclusive. As Richmond-Abbott (1983) states:

> While there may be some effect of sex hormones on the brain, we do not know whether sex hormones are really affecting the brain and, if they are, how they are exercising their effect. We do not know whether any effect begins at birth, is activated at puberty, or never exists at all (*Sex Roles over the Life Cycle, 67*).

A third theory about innate differences between the genders has to do with behavior. Males often are considered by virtue of their gender to be more aggressive, more competitive, and less nurturing than females. Studies that attempt to examine the relationship between sex hormones and aggression most often are conducted with animals. In the case of humans, however, it is very difficult to separate the effect of the environment from the innate factors some say affect behavior in humans. Taken as a body of research, studies done with human subjects tend to show no particular relationship between sex hormones and aggression. (Sadker, Sadker, & Klein 1991; Richmond-Abbott 1983)

Similarly, research regarding competition and nurturance in humans has found no particular link by gender that could be described as innate. Certainly, competitive and nurturing behavior are more likely to be found in males and females respectively, but many argue that these characteristics are learned within society, which values them in one gender or the other (Sadker, Sadker, & Klein 1991; Richmond-Abbott 1983).

Socialization Differences

Much social science research exists that examines gender differentiation as a result of socialization. A primary assumption is that our society, which is most heavily influenced by Western European culture, tends to hold gender stereotypes based on cultural tradition. For example, the tradition of the dominant culture in North America has been for males to take on roles that require instrumental characteristics. These characteristics, such as independence, assertiveness, and dominance, are also personality attributes that are valued in those in power positions in our society. On the other hand, expressive characteristics generally are assumed to be found more often in females. Dependence, passivity, and submission are traits valued for more nurturing or "feminine" activities, rather than for those in decision-making positions (Csikszentmihaly 1988).

While traditional views of masculinity and femininity are losing some of their rigidity, the presence of gender bias in our society remains and seems to affect career choices. Despite the fact that women constitute 42 percent of the work force in the United States, they remain substantially under-represented in government, corporate life, and other positions of decision-making power. Similarly, men represent a very small percentage of nurses, elementary teachers, and primary parents and/or homemakers. There are virtually no male preschool teachers (Tittle, in Klein 1985). It is, in part, a traditional view of appropriate roles for females and males that drives us to expect certain things of people according to their gender. This view suggests that gender-related behavioral traits are social constructions.

Perhaps the best-known studies that suggested gender traits are socially constructed were those conducted by Margaret Mead in 1935. Mead believed that cultural relativism (attitudes and characteristics of groups of people, in this case gender groups, according to the cultural group) was the contributing factor for the assumption of gender roles and traits rather than biological differences within a society.

Mead (1935) studied three primitive tribes in New Guinea. She found that the Mountain Arapesh men and women shared equally in the major occupation of the tribe, which was "growing things: children, pigs, and coconut trees" (Muuss 1988, p. 152). Mead described both gender groups in the tribe according to gender traits that typically refer only to females in Western culture: warm, peaceful, and caring about the needs of others.

In contrast, Mead's study of the Mundugumor of the Yuat River revealed people who, regardless of gender, displayed characteristics that traditionally are considered masculine. This tribe, who were cannibals, spent most of their time hunting. In their quest, both men and women displayed aggressiveness, competitiveness, and ruthless disregard for the needs of others, particularly children. In fact, Mead described child bearing and rearing as tasks that women particularly disliked. Mead saw no displays of "maternal instinct."

The third tribe Mead studied was the Lake-dwelling Tchambuli, in which she found yet another set of gender characteristics that varied considerably from those typically found in Western culture. These people depended on fishing and bartering for sur-vival. Women did nearly all of the labor. Mead described the women as "stern, dominant, matter-of-fact, and impersonal" (Muuss 1988, 154). The function of men was predominantly ornamental. They spent most of their time decorating themselves, creating dances, and planning ceremonies. Mead described them as "submissive, emotionally dependent, involved in petty bits of insult and gossip, less responsible than the women, but more responsive to the needs of others" (Muuss 1988, 154).

Mead's work in these cases provided examples of cultures in which gender role characteristics were well defined, yet quite dif-ferent from tribe to tribe as from many other cultures. She believed her research pointed to the conclusion that gender roles and the expectations we associate with them are a cultural phe-nomenon rather than a biological one.

Much of Mead's work has been criticized over the years. For example, in *Margaret Mead and Samoa: The Making and Unmak-ing of an Anthropological Myth* (1983), Freeman asserts that Mead's findings regarding Samoan youth, adolescence, and culture overall were patently false. The findings from his six-year study (compared to Mead's nine-month stay in Samoa) suggest Mead's conclusions were erroneous. Unfortunately, having died in 1978, Mead was unable to defend her conclusions. Regardless of the degree of merit one attributes to Mead's work in New Guinea and Samoa, she set the stage for researchers who study human develop-ment and the attainment of gender roles through a perspective of socialization rather than the perspective that biology is destiny.

Much research has been conducted that addresses issues of gender stereotyping and gender bias from a theoretical frame-work of socialization as the principal factor determining gender differentiation in our society. Other research seeks to explain the issue by providing biological evidence of gender differences driven by hormones and/or brain differences. The nature-versus-nurture controversy is certainly not settled. The prevailing wisdom is that an individual's development is influenced by a combination of environmental and biological factors. The explanation as to what causes human differences, for example between gender groups, is elusive due to the complexity of the issue and the endless variables involved.

Perhaps a more interesting part of this issue of male and female differences is not so much the cause of perceived differences but that the issue is a point of contention at all. In fact, recent education research indicates little significant variation between genders in academic achievement areas such as math and reading, while considerable variation exists within each gender group in these areas (Hyde & Linn 1986). Even though the research indicates that actual performance differences by gender appear to be minimal and possibly to be decreasing in some academic areas, many continue to think of males and females as being very different. This "differentiated gender thinking" can become gender bias and have detrimental effects on students in classrooms.

The complexity and subtlety of gender bias affects all aspects of classroom life for students. Who dominates the classroom; who interacts more often with the teacher; who generates more learning opportunities; and who is disciplined more frequently are all issues that direct one to the principal issue of who in general is empowered as a learner. One way to structure your thinking about gender issues in your classroom is by developing your understanding of gender equity as an issue of equal inputs or equitable outcomes. The following discussion examines these concepts.

GENDER EQUITY: EQUAL OR EQUITABLE?

Gender equity and related goals can be thought of as working to enhance the aspirations, achievement, talents, and interests of all students independent of their gender (*New Pioneers,* 1975). If asked, most teachers would report that they do their best to meet this general goal. However, approaching gender equity with such a broad, vague statement may result in business as usual, that is, with gender issues not being addressed critically by the teacher. In order to understand how gender equity might work for you in your own classroom, it is important to think through the broader concept of gender equity first, then carefully examine how it can be implemented through your teaching.

The label *gender equity* is used fairly universally to represent ways of thinking and acting that address gender issues. The term *equity* is used to describe the general concept. However, when one begins to consider how gender equity is operationalized, it becomes clear that there are essentially two ways to conceptualize it: within a framework of *equal* (or *equality,* when the term is used as a noun) or within a framework of *equitable.* Gender equity is the general term for referring to gender-related practices, but it may be interpreted as *equal* treatment or *equitable* treatment. Although perhaps confusing initially, it is important to differentiate between the terms.

In using the conceptual framework of equality, one is particularly concerned about issues at the beginning, or schooling "inputs," which Secada (1989) defines as

> what a school starts with when educating its students. Those resources—financial (monies), physical (books in a library, science lab equipment), and personnel (its teachers and how qualified they are)—are distributed (i) directly among schools and (ii) indirectly among the students who enroll in those schools (*Equity in Education, 70*).

The actions of implementing "equal" treatment would involve assuring that students receive the same opportunities for access and participation. A teacher could put this into practice by providing the same or equivalent materials to all learners; being certain all learners participate actively and with the same frequency; assuring that all learners receive equal access to aspects of the curriculum and assuring that all curriculum materials have comparable "male" and "female" characteristics or models. The operative words here are "same," "equal," and "equivalent." Teaching that is sensitive to gender equity practices and that is structured through this conceptual framework is concerned primarily with giving all students, female and male, an equal footing at the start. The idea is to allot all students the *same* level of instruction, attention, and expectation at the beginning (Secada 1989).

Several points are implied through this framework. An approach of equality will enhance the learning opportunities of female and male students. How equal the achievement or attitudes and dispositions of the students will be at the end of the period is fairly open ended. The implication is that with an equal beginning, students will proceed according to their individual capabilities. Some will do better than others or will have different preferences, but there will not be an explicit difference between identifiable groups (Secada 1989).

Gender equity through an "equitable" framework is approached differently. Its premise is that a particular group historically and habitually has been less advantaged within the system than another group. In the case of those committed to teaching equitably within the context of gender concerns, the group at risk is generally considered to be female learners, although there are certain circumstances within classroom life where it becomes quite clear that some males individually are the victims of gender bias. But when considering students as members of particular groups, females are arguably less advantaged when the final outcomes of academic achievement are measured (AAUW Report, 1992). Indeed, final outcomes tend to be the principal issue of concern when one adopts the framework of "equitable" as opposed to "equal." For instance, a teacher may stress participation of female learners in science over that for male learners if, for example, fewer females enter a science fair or score as highly on science tests as males. Another example of an approach according to an equitable framework might be a teacher who intentionally presses female students more than male students in math, if the teacher believes or has evidence that the female students are not achieving as well as the males. These are two curricula areas that have long been considered male domains. To try to meet the goal of similar achievement in science or math, the teacher practicing equitably begins by consciously acknowledging that one group is at risk for not achieving as well as the other group.

The next step of implementing gender equity through an equitable framework is to enhance opportunities for the at-risk group, sometimes to the point of extending an unequal and greater amount of resources toward that group rather than equalizing the resources between girls and boys. The rationale is that it is fair to work in a somewhat unequal fashion in order to remove the factors that have previously placed this group at risk for unequal achievement in the end. Gender-equitable teaching suggests that without extra or different consideration a particular group will not have the capability and opportunity to finish at the same level as the other group. Equal distribution of inputs, or resources such as quality of instruction, frequency of teacher interaction, and level of teacher expectation, is not sufficient to assure that there will be no significant difference between groups, female and male, when final outcomes are measured. While there is bound to be a range of achievement within each gender category, the ranges for both genders ought to have comparable distributions. Equitable teaching practices cannot assure the same outcomes for all individuals within a category, due to issues such as individuals' interests and levels of motivation. However, the goal is to attempt to provide for the possibility of equal outcomes given systematic societal biases.

Several problems are inherent in either approach. The principal problem with an approach to gender equity according to a framework of equality may be that, despite the assurances of equal access and equal participation, substantial achievement and participation differences may continue to exist between the genders. Even though one carefully considers the equal distribution of resources at the beginning, a significant difference by gender may continue to be present in many learning situations at the end. Many would argue that an equal approach is simply not sufficient to correct the effects of gender bias that prevail in society at large.

Taking up gender-sensitive teaching practices according to the equitable concept also is problematic. Intentionally diverting more resources to one group over another may be a difficult action for a teacher to take. There is a strong tendency for a teacher to do his or her best with each student; in a sense treating each student the same is one of the ethical standards that guide teachers and lead them to believe that they are doing the best thing for all students. There is a sense that it would be unfair to single out a particular group for special attention on a consistent basis. The traditional approach is to focus on the inputs and not to consider the broader issue of final outcomes.

A second dilemma inherent in teaching according to an equitable interpretation of gender equity is the reliance upon a teacher's correct assessment of the impact of societal biases in the classroom and in society. The implicit danger is that the teacher may actually do more harm than good through a skewed interpretation of the extent of gender bias. Teacher practice that reflects an extreme interpretation of gender bias (for example, denying its existence or overcompensating for its presence), may result in sexist or reverse-sexist practices. In the final analysis it may be impossible to determine that which is absolutely non-sexist, either in teaching practice or in one's analysis of society. The attempt to do so constitutes a struggle that teachers committed to equitable teaching must pursue.

How then does one integrate gender equity into teaching practice—according to an equal or equitable framework? In the following introductions of the teachers who are profiled throughout the book, you will note that six of the teachers put their commitment to gender equity into practice in their classrooms according to an equal framework of equality, while only one does so through an equitable framework. The analysis of Karen's teaching suggests that she may use a combination of the frameworks. The teachers demonstrate their beliefs about and understanding of gender equity practice in their own fashion. All are committed to addressing gender bias in their teaching, but their philosophies and methods vary. In order to gain a greater insight into how gender equity may be practiced in the classroom, the experiences, insights, and daily activities of these teachers will be integrated throughout the book.

In many ways, these teachers are quite typical. They deal with the same problems as teachers everywhere. Severe economic straits plague some of their schools; some teach in culturally diverse schools with students of low socioeconomic levels and with high dropout and pregnancy rates. Several teachers cope with upper middle-class parents who place extraordinary demands on them. These teachers face the same constraints as their colleagues. They are similar to the "average" teacher in other ways—they come from middle-class backgrounds, have traditional teacher training, and none is a person of color.

In other ways, the teachers are more than ordinary. All are considered highly successful teachers by their peers and principals. Their classrooms are well managed, and substantial learning takes place in them. But their most unusual characteristic, and the reason for their inclusion in this book, is their personal and professional commitment to gender equity to ensure that gender bias is not a part of their classroom teaching.

THE TEACHERS

The following introductions to the eight teachers' classroom practice will help illustrate different teaching approaches to, and even different understandings of, gender equity. As you come to know each teacher's perspective and situation, you may begin to develop a personal conception of gender equity as well as some ideas of how you may integrate equity considerations into your own teaching practice.

Each of the teachers was invited to participate in the work that informed the book. The most important factor in determining who was to be part of the project was commitment to gender equity in teaching. All of the teachers felt that they incorporate aspects of gender equity into their teaching practice to some degree.

I had known three of the teachers (Beth, Fred, and Bob) when they were graduate students in classes I taught. I was aware of their interest in gender issues in schools from our course activities. I came to know the other five teachers through my contacts with others. Judy, Karen, and Sean were identified as teachers interested in gender equity by a friend and colleague of mine.

I met Mary through a different set of circumstances. Several years prior to my work with this book, a student of mine in an undergraduate teacher preparation course spent a semester observing in Mary's classroom. In class discussions the student often spoke of gender equity-related practices Mary used in her classroom. Mary's principal assured me that I had found an excellent teacher who also placed a high priority on gender equity issues.

Pam's name was given to me by Tim Wernett, a staff person from a grant-supported project that provides, among other things, outreach services to teachers interested in implementing equity-related practices in their classrooms. Tim had known Pam for a number of years and felt she was a good example of a teacher who integrated gender equity into her classroom teaching. As I spent time talking with Pam and in her classroom, the recommendation for her participation in this work increasingly puzzled me. Pam's understanding of and interest in gender equity seemed fairly superficial to me, although she spoke of and demonstrated commitment to gender equity as a female issue, especially through her work in Planned Parenthood. During the initial stages of writing the book, I determined that Pam may reflect the way some teachers think of issues such as gender equity. She knows at some level that the issue is important to integrate into her teaching, but the myriad of other pressing concerns during her day take her time and attention. She is interested in, but cannot quite figure out how to integrate gender equity in ways other than those she currently uses. Because Pam's thinking is similar to that of many other teachers I have talked with over the years, I concluded that the information Pam provided, modest though it is, should remain in the text.

These eight people, who are considered effective teachers in general by their colleagues and/or principals and who are actively involved, to various degrees, in integrating gender equity into their teaching practice, provided the information upon which much of the book is based.

As you read through the chapters that describe the teachers, their classrooms, and their work with gender equity, it will be useful to keep several things in mind. None of the eight teachers was evaluated formally for either their teaching effectiveness in general or for their integration of gender equity into their teaching specifically. Therefore it is not possible to discuss any of them in terms of being an "expert." Further, in every case where it is presented, the analyses of their teaching is based on my interpretation, that of the teacher, or a combination. Each of the teachers reviewed the sections of the book that described him or her and confirmed that my interpretations were accurate. Nevertheless, it is conceivable that another individual would develop a different interpretation.

Finally, bear in mind that none of the teachers necessarily provides a "best" example of how to interpret gender equity or implement various methods to achieve it. You may find that one teacher does some thing correctly, as you see it, while another uses other methods or materials you like. Perhaps one of the teachers will represent the best of the lot to you. Taken together, these teachers provide a varied picture of "regular" teachers working with gender equity on a daily basis.

Judy's Preschool Class

Judy directs and teaches in a preschool in a medium-sized school district. Small by the standards of many other preschools, the preschool consists of four classes of a maximum of fourteen students each. Special-needs students (those who have been diagnosed as requiring different and extra attention in school due to a handicapping condition) are integrated with non-special needs children. Each classroom has a low adult-to-student ratio: about 1 to 4. A teacher, an aide, and a special education teacher comprise the staff for each class. This ratio is often lowered with the addition of parent volunteers. The socioeconomic composition of the preschool as well as the district overall is generally upper middle class. Very few students of color live in the district or attend the preschool.

Judy's interpretation of equity issues in general and gender equity in particular becomes evident when she speaks of her background.

> I grew up in a family that was very committed to social equality. My mother worked with the war on poverty. The efforts my

parents went to; I can remember being a pre-schooler, going to a dentist on the other end of town. My mother wanted me to see a black professional. That was how she could make that happen. I came of age emotionally in the counterculture. Gender equity was part of that.

Judy also credits parental values and messages received at home for shaping her beliefs.

I'm not somebody who had lots of experiences with frustration with being female and how that has created limits for me. I was born into a family that preferred girls, so I got to be the pre-ferred gender. I had a professional mother, so it was always expected I would go through college and I would be a profes-sional.

Judy's personal experiences as a child and adolescent within the context of her family helped shape her perceptions about her abilities and aspirations. From those experiences as well as others as an adult, Judy has constructed her beliefs about equity. While gender equity is an important issue to Judy, she considers it one of secondary importance to the issues of equity in general. She per-ceives culture and class conflicts as the broader topics. As these equity concerns are addressed in her teaching, she believes gender issues also should be examined by the students. When one deals with the concept of equity effectively, the goal is to sensitize the student to bias in any form, whether cultural, class, or gender. Therefore, as Judy endeavors to open the minds of her three-, four-, and five-year-olds, she attempts to do so in a way that bias of any kind eventually will be apparent to the student.

There are several aspects of Judy's understanding of gender equity that are unique among this group of teachers. While she shares the framework of equality with a number of the other teachers, her teaching illustrates the most gender neutral practice of all of the teachers. As you will note in chapter 5, in which teacher interactions are discussed, Judy attempts to and succeeds in working with both girls and boys in nearly an identical fashion. Her tone of voice and her words are as similar from one child to the next as she can possibly make them. Judy is the most clear-cut example of the practice of gender neutrality, or commitment to equal inputs.

Another aspect of Judy's interpretation of gender equity that should be pointed out as different from that of the other teachers is her steadfast resistance to using what she calls "propaganda." When faced with a situation where a student is clearly demonstrating gender bias, Judy does not directly instruct the child in the "correct" way of thinking or behaving. Instead she enters into a dialogue with the child, questioning him or her about assumptions and how he or she came to a particular way of thinking or acting. She calls this creating "cognitive conflict." She believes that if she can open the way for the child to consider alternative or additional information, when faced with a similar situation at another time, the child may choose to take a different course of action or think differently with regard to bias. Because Judy does not insist on the child coming away from such a discussion with her perspective or way of thinking, many of these dialogues are left somewhat open-ended. A teacher who is not so convinced of the eventual effectiveness of this approach might be uneasy with the lack of closure and assurance that the child understands the point. Judy, however, is confident that this subtle and non-confrontational method is the most productive means of creating change in biased attitudes in the long run. She is similarly committed to incorporating a gender-equity framework of equality in her teaching.

Karen's Kindergarten

Karen teaches kindergarten in a primary magnet school (a voluntary desegregation site), which encompasses kindergarten through third grade students. She has worked in the school since its transition to a magnet school in 1978. The school is in a low-socioeconomic neighborhood with a nearly 100 percent ethnic minority population, drawing half its population from the neighborhood and the other half from voluntary transfer students who must identify themselves as white and non-Hispanic. The population of the school is heterogeneous, culturally and socioeconomically. Karen's kindergarten students mirror the mixture of the school as a whole—half are neighborhood children and half are voluntary transfer children.

Karen believes her most difficult struggles in working with bias in the classroom have to do with class distinction and gender issues. Both of these concerns certainly have to do with equity issues in general, but Karen considers them as distinct entities that should be directly and separately addressed. In a very real sense, she teaches her students about gender issues and gender stereotypes. She believes that gender bias comes from many directions, principally the family and the media. But she also recalls some situations from her own schooling experience that she says reflected gender bias.

> Boys got to do the important things. Girls got to do the unimportant things, except in the month of May. In Catholic school the month of May was Virgin Mary's month. Girls got to carry the flag, but we still didn't get to light candles or carry the host to the alter. In high school, boys got to play sports and we didn't, except intramural sports. It wasn't until college that we got to really compete.

In reflecting on these experiences and others, she describes her goal of teaching with equity in mind:

> I'm not sure any of these experiences shaped my current commitment toward gender equity directly at the time. Understanding gender equity was a later acquisition for me. I certainly wanted to make sure there was more fairness around in general.

Much of Karen's interpretation of gender equity can be described as stemming from the framework of equality. While she does not equalize her interactions with her students to the extent that Judy does, she is sensitive about equal access and equal opportunity for males and females. She also is not reticent about nudging her students into particular learning situations if their own preconceived gender biases might deter them. Karen describes her actions this way:

> I will structure it so that all children will have a time specifically with the blocks, for example. Some kids will stake out certain areas and other kids won't go in. Sometimes that's based on gender. Some kids have more familiarity with some things; with blocks or the coloring table. So I structure it at the beginning of the year so that all kids have a chance to get in there. Sometimes I will say, "You know, I haven't seen girls over here for ages," or when we're sitting down, I'll say, "Look at how we're sitting. Is this how we want to sit, girls on one side and boys on the other?"

Karen is concerned with making sure that no student is excluded from any learning or socializing opportunity. She also works from the beginning to make sure her students understand what bias and exclusion mean. To that end, not long after the school year is under way, Karen's students often talk about gender issues within the context of their work and play. They demonstrate a sensitivity to gender-bias situations such as very few females portrayed in literature and stereotyped ideas about career opportunities. If one inadvertently should use the pronoun "he" in a generic sense, the children are likely to correct the sexist language.

Karen makes the learners in her classroom active participants in identifying gender bias and uncovering gender-based stereotypes. She is neither subtle nor confrontational, but direct and insistent in her approach. This method, coupled with her framework of equality of opportunity and equivalent distribution of resources works for Karen in meeting her goal of addressing gender equity in her teaching practice.

Mary's Third Grade

Mary has taught third grade in Judy's school district for several years. The same homogeneous quality permeates the elementary school as the preschool; the students for the most part are upper middle-class and white, non-Hispanic. As part of the third-grade team, Mary works within a prescribed curriculum in the content areas. However, despite considerable constraints on time available to deviate from what must be taught, Mary is able to weave threads of gender equity into her teaching. Mary carefully chooses curriculum materials that depict females in areas where they typically are not shown. The use of enrichment materials that intentionally provide a gender balance is one example of Mary's approach to gender equity. In providing materials that display males and females occupied in all activities during any given point in history, Mary is demonstrating her interpretation of gender equity through a framework of equality. To make up for a lack of female characters in the required literature for her class, she inserts readings that do incorporate females. A more balanced representation of males and females is created; the students are exposed to works that portray females as main characters as well those in which male characters dominate. By choosing enriching materials that incorporate female as well as male figures and through other techniques, Mary works to enhance the experiences of all of her students through an understanding of gender equity that focuses on inputs and processes that are meant to provide equal opportunity.

Perhaps more than the other teachers, Mary believes her personal experiences have shaped her commitment to addressing

gender equity in her teaching. In reflecting upon her own schooling experiences, she remembered this:

> Boys were treated really differently. I remember that. For six-
> teen years I wanted to be a boy; they were treated so differently.
> They had all kinds of advantages, certainly in sports and P.E.
> and things like that. They were also regarded as the scientists.
> That involved more hands-on. And they were definitely seen as
> the mathematicians a lot more than the girls. Although we had
> our math program, it wasn't very exciting. The boys were seen
> as more capable. They were also seen as more mischievous, and
> that was more appealing than always being goody-good.

Aside from curricular issues and teacher expectations of academic ability that she recalls as gender biased, she also remembers
gender differences in how discipline was handled.

> I went to schools where children were disciplined by hitting
> them. I was not hit. Even when I'd do relatively awful things.
> Like in junior high I stole a grade book and I wasn't even sus-
> pected. Had I been a boy, I would have been suspected. Another
> time I brought a toad. It really frightened the teacher. I wasn't
> disciplined the way I would have been had I been a boy.

In summing up her memories of her schooling and the impact
it has brought to her teaching practice, Mary says simply, "I
would like to believe I'm more equitable."

Sean's Middle School Art Classes

Of the teachers in the group, Sean has taught school the longest.
He began teaching art in elementary school. Ten years later, he
moved to middle school, where he has worked with early adoles-
cents for twenty years. The school is in a middle-class neighborhood but reflects a fairly broad socioeconomic range due to
mandatory busing as part of a school district desegregation plan.

The principal of the middle school referred to Sean as "Mr.
Workshop" when contacted for permission to observe Sean's
classes. The affectionate nickname refers to Sean's interest in constantly renewing his teaching, which he does in part through participation in workshops and other types of training. One area of
particular interest for Sean over the past several years has been gender equity. He participated in the Gender Expectations and Student
Achievement (GESA) project (Grayson & Martin 1988) several

years ago, and since then has worked to integrate gender equity into his classroom practice. To some extent Sean believes his personal background helped shape his awareness of gender issues.

> Elementary school was a three-room schoolhouse on the south rim of the Grand Canyon. We were pretty much self-segregated [by gender]on the playground. As far as the classroom goes, my impression is we were treated pretty equally; except I felt that some of the girls got more attention. That was probably because they got better grades. In high school, we were definitely separated. I went to a mission high school in Utah. I know shop was definitely a boys' class and cooking was definitely a girls' class. Several of the boys wanted to take cooking and some of the girls wanted to take shop. They definitely wouldn't let that happen.

In thinking back about anything in his schooling experience that might have been particularly good or bad because of his gender, Sean said:

> It was probably in high school. It was a sense of not being one of the group because I didn't participate in the sports activities. Two of us didn't. Leonard and I both convinced the coach that in the winter, rather than take tumbling, something else that we could do was chip the ice off the sidewalk. We said it would be good exercise and good for the school. He let us, and we passed P.E. I was looking forward to the sports program; I wanted to participate. I knew I needed the exercise. But I certainly couldn't match up to the coach's expectations of what was needed on a team. So I definitely was not one of the locker room jocks. I wound up in speech and debate instead. I think because of these experiences I'm more accepting of students who don't conform to some form of preset convention as far as what's expected of them.

Sean experienced exclusion due to preconceived notions of what boys should be able to do, on the part of the teacher or, in the case above, the coach. These experiences have influenced Sean in the way he thinks about gender issues with regard to his students. Sean's perceptions about fairness and his sensitivity are demonstrated in the classes he teaches through an equal framework.

Sean's work with gender equity is done principally through methods of classroom management. While this includes discipline, it focuses on teacher-to-student interactions, monitoring practices, and careful lesson planning. Sean does not teach directly about anything that remotely could be considered a gender issue, nor does he shape any of his interactions with students along a gender theme. Instead he is primarily concerned with equalizing access and opportunities to succeed in the classes he teaches.

In a fashion somewhat similar to Judy's, Sean attempts to work with students in an even, equivalent way. His method of interaction is to question and critique, giving each student an equal allotment of his instructional time and attention. He structures his classes so that even the least motivated student can be cajoled into achieving success through completion of the art projects. Largely due to his own level of energy and constant monitoring, he is able to keep all students on task so they virtually have no choice but to finish and succeed.

Fred's Middle-School Social Studies Classes

Fred has taught middle-school social studies for twelve years in his present school, which is culturally and socioeconomically diverse. The social studies curriculum, which Fred helped develop some years ago, focuses directly on issues of racial/ethnic and gender equity. Careful attention is given to varied points of view by culture and gender groups within the prescribed curriculum. This is Fred's principal means of addressing gender equity. A secondary method he uses is *equal* monitoring and questioning. Analysis of the two indicate that Fred's understanding of gender equity is that of identical treatment of females and males. He works to be sure that students, regardless of gender, are represented in the curriculum materials. He also meticulously includes every student in his questioning sessions and during periods of monitoring. Fred is not effusive in his interactions with his students. The interactions are confined to the task at hand. Indeed, he runs a tight ship and maintains momentum throughout class sessions.

Fred shares some characteristics with Judy in implementing gender-equity methods. He relies on the capabilities of his students to take in the information and then figure out the implications or what the different perspectives mean to them. He does not choose materials or methods through which he directly confronts the students about gender bias in their words or behavior. When asked if he would intervene in a situation outside the classroom if exclusion by gender was taking place, say in a game, he responded:

If the girls were being excluded, I would let the boys know the girls could play if they wanted to and try to achieve a balance that way. If the situation was an informal, impromptu gathering, I might not intervene. As opposed to intervening, I might say, "Don't you want to play over here or start another game?"

Fred is hesitant to impose his values on the students in informal educational situations in which he believes it is his duty as a teacher to provide equal opportunities. Instead he suggests that the situation may not be fair and proposes that the students figure out the solution. The sense of open-endedness and allowing the students to make the choice for themselves is similar to Judy's dislike for propaganda and for telling the students what they should do.

Fred also considers gender equity when he chooses enrichment materials for classroom use. A number of simulations, many dealing with cultural and gender issues, are an important part of Fred's curriculum. He chooses the simulations based on their ability to expose students to other points of view and what he describes as the subtly of their approach.

I try to use things that aren't real heavy handed. They aren't simulations that hit someone over the head; rather they're things that give a different look, say, at a period of time or at government, from someone else's point of view.

Fred's perspective of gender equity is that of *equalizing* the curriculum, through materials that equally represent males and females and through carefully providing the same amount of instructional attention to the girls and boys in his classes. Fred believes that his primary role as a teacher is to ensure that information is provided for the students. If the material is equal in its representation of the genders, then it is left to the student to make sense of the information. Fred provides the information and some of the questions. The students must provide the cognition that will allow them to interpret and form their own opinions and values. Direct intervention or interaction that relates specifically to gender issues would be appropriate only in a setting where it was required to assure *equal inputs*, and that in a formal schooling situation.

Beth's Middle-School Science Classes

Beth clearly remembers several episodes from her own schooling that influenced her commitment to and understanding of gender equity.

I was in the ninth grade when the feminist movement started. All the language-arts teachers blocked language arts. All three of them were very encouraging in equity ways. They pointed out inequities to us. They were really strong, NOW members, which at the time was a radical organization. And they really encouraged the girls to speak up and out. We did simulations and that way got a chance to voice a lot of opinions. On the negative side, I was such a jock and athlete. I remember in grade school teachers really getting angry at me when I would go outside at recess, instead of stay in and do art work. They had little volunteer things to do I never wanted to do. I think they would call my mom sometimes: "She just runs out at the bell." Even though I was an A student. And I don't think they would have done that to a boy.

I remember the complete lack of counseling. I just always took what my sister took. Fortunately she was a serious academician, more math and science. I never was encouraged to take any of them.

These experiences played a part in shaping Beth's aggressive, proactive ideas about gender equity in her role as a teacher. Beth's work in dealing with gender issues far exceeds the boundaries of her classroom. As described in Chapter 4, she has developed programs designed to counter what she considers cultural and general societal barriers to success for the young women in her school at large. The breadth of Beth's work with gender equity within the context of her role as a teacher is much greater than any of the other teachers in this group.

Another characteristic that sets her apart is the *equitable* framework she has adopted. Beth is concerned primarily with outcomes and secondarily with inputs. She believes that female students in her classes and the school are more at risk than the boys because of pervasive societal gender bias. Based on this belief, Beth consciously distributes her resources unevenly; her instructional time and attention and her energy outside of the classroom are directed more to the girls than the boys. In order to enhance girls' opportunities for success in her science classroom and in the schooling process from middle school onward, Beth overcompensates in her approach to them in an attempt to equalize the eventual outcomes. This is not to say that the boys are systematically ignored; they are a strong presence in the classes. But Beth is very conscious of the tendency in any classroom for male domination, particularly in a domain such as science, which typically is perceived to be masculine. She controls for the dominance and, on balance, demands more participation of her female students than of her male students. When asked the question, If your resources as a teacher are limited, should one group (gender) receive more than the other? a respondent replying from a perspective of *equality* would certainly say no, from the perspective of wanting to make everything within the learning situation the same for each student. However, an equitable framework would dictate an answer of yes, with at least slightly more than half of the resources directed toward the oppressed or at risk-group. Beth's response to the question was immediate.

> Girls ought to get it. Of course. Although during the Women's Month activities, I wish there was something for boys. But I always find my interest and concern are for the girls.

There is some tension apparent in her response. On the one hand, Beth has a strong commitment as a teacher to be certain that all her students receive her best. However, her belief in the importance of gender equity through an equitable framework takes a dominant position in her general perspective of how to go about empowering all her students in the long run.

Pam's High-School Health Class

Pam has taught senior health classes at a lower-middle to middle-class, principally white (non-Hispanic) high school for several years. Pam might be described as a teacher whose commitment to gender equity in her teaching is still forming and gradually emerging. Of the eight teachers she may give the least amount of conscious reflection to gender issues. She states although she is interested, she probably doesn't know enough about gender equity to be doing it all "right." Yet she is concerned enough to ensure that several aspects of her teaching practice reflect attempts to deal with gender issues. Her primary method of addressing gender equity is through her curriculum. She concentrates on providing information about health issues that affect males and females, not necessarily both. For example, she provides time during her nine-week class sessions for all students to learn about eating disorders. She also discusses testicular cancer. Pam attempts to balance her curricular offerings so important issues for females that might not be of concern to males will be addressed, as well as the reverse. Pam interprets gender equity through a framework of equality.

> I don't really see any difference between the girls and the guys. I don't particularly plan for it (gender equity) and I don't treat them any differently.

While she does not remember any particular events in her background that might have directly influenced her decision to be concerned about gender issues in the classroom, she does tie it to her earlier work with women.

> I can't recall anything about my own school experiences about how girls and boys might have been treated differently. And there was nothing in my teacher training which dealt with it. My interest in gender equity started when I met a friend at Planned Parenthood. He worked there when I volunteered there. My interest is based pretty much on the fact that he was interested, and our friendship.

Of the eight teachers, Pam shows the least amount of active interest and reflection regarding gender equity. For that reason, she provides an important example for prospective and practicing teachers to consider. As a fairly new teacher in a school that carefully scrutinizes its teachers for their competence in areas such as time on task and other behavioral or immediately measurable kinds of teacher functions, Pam feels pressure to do things that are most essential for her evaluation by the principal. When asked about her feelings or ideas about aspects of gender equity in her teaching, Pam states:

> I'm not too aware of them. I haven't gotten that sophisticated. I'm too busy.

With no previous training or compelling personal experiences that shaped her commitment to gender equity, Pam and other novice teachers like her may find it difficult to focus on gender equity as an essential issue to be integrated into teaching practice on more than a superficial level. Her daily concerns about some of the more routine administrative tasks may provide too much competition for her attention. This is a common complaint with novice teachers who may not have had the opportunity to learn how to reflect about what and how they teach. Pam knows there are important considerations that she may not be addressing in her teaching and acknowledges that gender equity is one of them. She pays attention to several aspects of the issue but has not yet given serious thought to how gender issues play out in the classroom.

Bob's High-School Biology Classes

Bob has taught high-school science for a number of years. The school where he currently teaches has approximately 25 percent ethnic minority, middle-class students. Bob seems by nature a reflective person, about his teaching practice and his life in general. He provides rich memories of his background, which he says shaped his commitment to gender equity.

> I went to an all-boys parochial high school, so that pretty much limited any kind of interaction between genders that I could talk about. But my grammar school days, grades 1–8 I definitely remember girls being treated differently. Boys were expected to be more assertive, boys were expected to be leader types, and girls were shuttled into subordinate roles and were given no encouragement as far as I could see to try to assert whatever talents they might have had in the direction of something nontraditional. I believe that I was indeed favored because I was a boy.

In considering how some of these experiences may influence his teaching, he remarks:

> Probably the absence of females in my own school experiences is the one item that reflects most heavily in my teaching. If anything, what it does is cause me to lavish more attention on females, although I try to make a concerted effort not to do that. Although I think that since I'm in an area that has traditionally been open to males and not females, perhaps it's good that I encourage females more.
>
> Because of the gender segregation in the high school where I went, I was dramatically socially retarded. It took most of my college career to figure out how to deal with a woman. Every relationship I was exposed to early on, it wasn't like I had to be real assertive or had something to prove, just the opposite—I was quite intimidated. I felt there was some standard I was supposed to live up to, and didn't have the experience. It's just like the situation where you deal with (ethnic) segregation versus integration. If you're allowed to work with members of minority groups, students realize you have true integration because these people are working together. Had I had the opportunity to

go to school with girls, I would have been much more comfortable with girls. It wouldn't have been a big deal. It would not have been something like, Oh, this is a girl. It would just have been, This is another person.

Bob's personal experiences in the past, particularly attending high school in an all-boys school, have stayed with him and helped foster his sensitivity toward gender issues in his teaching practice.

He is somewhat ambivalent about the framework within which he feels most comfortable approaching gender equity in the classroom. When he spoke of giving more attention to females in his classes, he also commented that he tries not to do so. On the other hand, he says that it may be acceptable after all, because females generally may be less likely to succeed in science than males. Bob's response to another question provided further insight into his apparent ambivalence. When asked if any instructional setting would be appropriate for males and females to be separated, with the goal of enhancing the opportunities or abilities of one group, Bob said:

> I think that might work from the standpoint of the girls being better able to compete, but it seems that a large portion of the problem of gender equity is the willingness of the males to accept females. If you segregate you may be addressing half of the problem (enhancing female skills by avoiding the potential of male dominance) but you're not addressing the other half, and that's the acceptance of the males. It would seem to me to be more effective to have them together and simply monitor sufficiently to make sure the girls get the opportunity to develop and build skills. At the same time you need to show the boys that girls are capable of manipulating these skills, so you really do address both sides of the problem. I quite frankly don't know which of the two sides of the problem are more serious. For example, there are some very talented women out there who can't get jobs because they will not be accepted by the males. And that may be the more serious aspect.

In thinking through the dilemma, Bob ultimately decides that different treatment, or in this case the separation of females from males in order to enhance females' opportunities, is not the best means of approaching gender equity. Instead, he supports the concept of providing *equal* resources and opportunities.

SUMMARY

The eight teachers' experiences and approaches to gender equity do vary. Some recall incidents that may have had a direct bearing on their interest in and commitment to gender equity, at least in hindsight. Some became aware of the importance of gender issues in their teaching much later, well into their adulthood when they were already teachers. Further, each interprets gender equity in an individual fashion. Most can be said to practice it in their classrooms within an equality framework. The exception is Beth, who demonstrates an approach that is clearly an equitable interpretation. Lastly, while all consciously reflect on gender equity and what it means in their teaching, they do so to varying degrees. It could be argued that Beth displays the most extensive commitment to gender equity. Dealing with gender issues permeates her thinking and actions in general and in her role as a teacher. On the other side of the continuum is Pam. She still is somewhat uncertain about her understanding of gender equity. She acknowledges her interest and its importance but is unclear about how to make gender equity an integral part of her teaching.

As you read about the various aspects of gender equity and discover how these eight teachers address them in distinctive ways, you should begin to understand how you—in your life and in your role as a teacher specifically—interpret gender equity.

A number of aspects of gender equity and its relationship to classroom teaching have been introduced. Specific attention is given to these issues in the chapters that follow. Problems seen in today's classrooms and pertinent research findings are discussed. Along with this information, you will see how the eight teachers incorporate gender equity into their teaching in order to counter these problems.

You should be aware of two additional points about the eight teachers. First, you will encounter only certain teachers in chapters 3–6. The teachers who provided the best examples in each aspect of gender equity discussed were selected for inclusion. You will become best acquainted with Judy, Karen, and Beth, because their practice of gender equity is the most comprehensive of the eight teachers.

A second point to bear in mind is that all of the teachers tended to construct their understanding of gender equity primarily as a female issue. While all included males in their discussions, the teachers generally focused their efforts on either making sure the girls in their classes received the same resources as the boys or, as in the case of Beth, that girls received more than boys.

As you read the research and examine the methods employed by the teachers to counter gender bias, you might agree that female learners as a group are more at risk within the schooling institutions, or perhaps you will conclude this perspective is problematic. Whichever understanding you develop, you will need to construct your interpretation of gender equity considering both the daily activities of teachers in their classrooms and the larger societal and political ramifications.

CHAPTER 2

Socialization

This chapter provides brief historical backgrounds of social and school structures and gender. A great deal has been written on each of these topics, but I have provided only the briefest of accounts, to familiarize the reader with essential information. Readers should refer to the cited sources or numerous others for a thorough discussion of the topics. Some familiarity with these topics should help the reader develop a greater understanding of gender bias in United States culture today.

SOCIAL STRUCTURE AND GENDER

In our society, as in nearly all others, gender roles play a large part in how we as individuals come to identify ourselves and how society judges us. Unfortunately, even though substantial numbers of females and males in our society are choosing nontraditional gender roles, traditional definitions of what it means to be male or female have not changed correspondingly. Further, rigid societal roles have a way of becoming attached to particular statuses, with some roles given higher value than others. In American society and in most others, masculine roles have higher status than those characterized as feminine (Richmond-Abbott 1983).

Our dominant culture has long held that the male role and characteristics that accompany it are associated with power and prestige, while the female role is considered a subservient one. The effect of strict gender roles on men and women is the loss of realized potential. Rigidly interpreted, these roles create the expectations that males at all costs aspire to and fulfill the masculine roles, while females are held back from any position that permits acquisition of power (Sadker and Sadker 1982).

One might argue that the women's movement and other mechanisms of gender related social reform have changed how society defines masculine and feminine. There is no question that increasing numbers of individuals over the past twenty years have chosen occupations that previously were the domain of the other gender. Similarly, in schools girls and boys are now able to participate in curricular areas that were not open to earlier generations of that gender. However, in general societal expectations based on gender remain fairly well entrenched, particularly with regard to the issue of status and power (Richardson & Taylor 1989).

Gender and role status have become inextricably tied; so much so that gender identity—one's sense of being male or female—is connected to one's work. If a man chooses a typically "female" occupation, he does so at the risk of appearing effeminate. The labels such as "male nurse" or "male secretary" are representative of society's hesitancy to allow men to do "women's work." Because men in these positions are an anomaly, we have created words that highlight the conflict between gender and a man's choice of work when the work is considered "feminine" (Richardson & Taylor 1989).

Women are much more likely to opt for "male" occupations than men are for "female" occupations. In "male" careers, women can hope to attain the status of the position. Yet they also must deal with the conflict of what society asserts is appropriate for females and the acquisition of male or instrumental characteristics required for competition and success. For women to succeed in men's work, they often find themselves down-playing their feminine characteristics and emphasizing more masculine traits. Instrumental traits, as opposed to expressive traits, are more likely to be valued and consistent with achievement in our society (Kessler-Harris 1989, in Richardson & Taylor).

In order to achieve roles that are in conflict with the prevailing gender stereotypes, an individual may in a sense be required to sacrifice some of the gender role identity he or she has developed during earlier years. Nonetheless, many do so. Why then, if substantial numbers of individuals opt for non-traditional occupations or ways of living, do the gender role stereotypes remain largely intact? The answer is derived in part from the tradition of earlier societies, from the influence of Judeo-Christian religion, from tradition that is uniquely American, and from social institutions such as our schools.

Early Society and Gender Role Stratification

Nearly every society, historically as well as currently, has some scheme of social stratification. The social stratum to which one belongs strongly influences one's power and prestige. Social status in industrialized nations is associated with such factors as material wealth, extent of formal schooling, occupational status, as well as the family into which one was born. But social stratification also is framed along gender lines. In nearly every society today as well as in the past, a person's gender plays some role in defining her or his social status as well as the particulars of the role the person will take on as an adult. Because social stratification is tied to gender, roles ascribed to one gender or the other take on a particular value in society. In nearly every society today, masculine social roles are more valued than feminine roles (Richmond-Abbott 1983).

Why do societies tend to make roles gender related? Additionally, how have we come to value roles traditionally held by males over those held by females? As described in chapter 1, several theories have been developed that attempt to tie gender-related traits to hormonal or other biological factors. To date, this research is too incomplete to support the contention, for example, that male students will do better in some academic areas because of innate factors or that females will be likely to behave in a particular fashion for biological reasons. Further, many consider the reasoning behind these theories of gender-specific innate abilities to be faulty. A powerful argument against biologically related differences can be found in some recent research. The work of Hyde & Linn (1986) indicates that, contrary to the traditionally held assumptions of gender-related differences in academic areas, only small statistically significant differences exist between the genders in content areas such as math. The larger differences are found within the gender groups. Regardless of the cause of gender role differences, the more interesting questions may be why one gender has tended to be valued over the other and why these notions persist. Differentiated gender roles and their societal value may have their origins in the first societies.

Because it is not possible to be certain about ancient cultural traditions, anthropologists can only theorize and speculate. Several interesting theories hypothesize about the inception of specific gender roles. Richmond-Abbott (1983) discusses the theories of Tanner and Zhilman (1976) and Zuckerman (1979), which examine pre-historic humans and the division of labor. Both theories center around the importance of the person who provided the most food to the group. Zuckerman (1979) suggests that male-female couples developed as a social pattern, with males dominant. Since the female needed to stay with needy infants she was dependent on the male to bring the food to her. Tanner and Zhilman (1976), however, see the female as dominant in the fledgling culture. They speculate that as a gatherer (rather than hunter) of food, the female was responsible for between half to almost all of the food gathering. They contend that she was also the one who probably was responsible for creating implements that enriched the culture. As Richmond-Abbott (1983) points out, it is a matter of interpretation as to which gender was providing the most valuable service. But what is clear is that specific roles were defined by gender very early in the process of civilization.

As the importance of technology advanced, with strength and physical presence becoming decreasingly necessary for survival, the status of males and the specificity of their roles persisted. Sanday (1981) gives an interesting example of this within the context of changing cultures.

> When the Dutch opened gold mines in South Africa, African men got the jobs that gave them cash and power. In other cases the role of women in planting and raising crops was ignored, and new seed, plows, and fertilizer were given to the men, who then raised surpluses that gave them power. Thus, men worked for cash or controlled the production of exchange crops, and women were left with raising food for the family and with household chores (in Richmond-Abbott 1983, 9).

The issue of the continual domination of males in societies throughout recorded history remains a bit of a mystery. Rosaldo (1980) suggests that inasmuch as historical records were written by men, male contribution and power might have been overemphasized. Men's public roles, as documented in the records, may have been portrayed in a distorted way. However, these records are what we have to study and make assumptions from concerning the lives of people in early societies. It is easy to see how these records could be taken at face value and where our interpretation of long-lived male role domination in societies, accurate or not, may come from.

Theories of the sources of specific gender roles can be summarized according to the categories of reproduction and child care, production of food, division of labor, and control of the environment (Richmond-Abbott 1983). Men of course were participants in reproduction, but not in child care, and they probably controlled the production of a great amount of food as well. Labor came to be divided in gender specific ways, and men were perceived as controlling the environment, particularly in times of war. Lastly, male roles of early recorded civilizations can be described as public and they are well recorded. Public roles tend to be celebrated while private ones, which were most often the domain of women, are not. Historical records provide documentation and celebration of men's roles, while women's accomplishments and lives are undocumented and largely invisible.

Religion and Gender

Religion also has had substantial influence on the creation and, especially, the maintenance of gender roles. Most religions have underscored the superiority of males and the inferiority of females. This is due in part to a long history of the worship of primarily male deities. However, it is interesting to note that not all early religions were male dominated (Richmond-Abbott 1983).

Early religious records of the beginnings of religion indicate that both male and female deities were worshipped. Some anthropologists believe that the worship of female deities and matriarchal societies was found in the earliest forms of culture (Maccoby, 1971). Others suggest that, while perhaps not the first construction of society, matriarchies did dominate at a point in early history. Vaerting and Vaerting (1923, in Bullough 1974, 21) provide an example of gender roles in one such society.

> In states ruled by women, the man contributed a dowry and had to be faithful over the period of the marriage. Women were entitled to divorce their partners if they were no longer pleased by them, and they could also dispose of any common possessions. The husband adopted the name and nationality of his wife, adorned himself in fancy clothes, and was considered as somewhat less intelligent but more sociable than the female.

Eastern and western religions have long histories of differentiating the roles and views of the genders. While Islam, Buddhism, and Hinduism differ in many doctrines and rituals, all prescribe lower status for women. In early societies that were theocracies, the religious laws usually dictated that women had few rights and little protection under the law. With the advent of Judaism male figures took on dominant roles, and females were denigrated. For example, women's sexuality came to be associated with evil, and traditions and rituals were established whereby women periodically were isolated from the rest of the community. Richmond-Abbott (1983, 17) cites a number of Old Testament passages that illustrate the prevailing view of women:

If a woman conceives and bears a male child, then she shall be unclean for several days . . . but if she bears a female child then she shall be unclean for two weeks (Leviticus 12:2–5).

How can he be clean that was born of a woman (Job 4:4)?

It is good for a man not to touch a woman . . . Nevertheless to avoid fornication, let every man have his own wife, and let every woman have her own husband (Corinthians 7:1–2).

By 300 A.D. worship of Mary as a symbol of female virginity and sexual purity had become popular. In addition, Mary's role in relationship to Jesus came to be interpreted as that of a nurturing, warm, and loving mother. The image of the perfect woman came to be that of virginal purity, while she also produced children to whom she would attend with kindness, warmth, and love. These characteristics ascribed to women linger as qualities that many societies continue to hold as descriptive of the ideal woman (Richmond-Abbott 1983).

With the beginnings of Protestantism the status of women improved. As prescribed by doctrine, individuals were believed to communicate directly with God, in the case of women as well as men. Although they were not allowed positions in the church, women took on slightly higher status from their previous position of unclean possessions. A conflict arose, however, between this improved status and entrenched expectations for female behavior. Any actions that might be construed as assertive or disobedient could be considered grounds for charges of being a witch. Witch burnings occurred in Europe and early America during the seventeenth century, when thousands of women lost their lives due to their deviance from or inability to conform to the appropriate gender role and its prescribed behavior (Richmond-Abbott 1983). Many religions, ancient and modern, have helped contribute to and maintain gender role stratification.

Gender Roles in Early North America

Early European immigrants to North America brought much of their tradition and heritage with them, including their views of appropriate gender roles. However, circumstances different from those in Europe contributed to the beginnings of slightly different interpretations of gender roles of women. Many women in early North America took on nearly all roles within the community. Depending on their location, women produced food, made necessary commodities for the home, provided armed defense for the settlement, and raised children. They often were a vital part of the economy and therefore held higher status than their counterparts in cultures where females did not participate in such activities. Perhaps because there were proportionately few women in the developing areas, they were remarkably mobile. Women often moved to locations that lacked females. This mobility had the effect of giving them more autonomy; however as the regions became more populated, the relative freedom of women diminished and their roles became more limited (Hill 1967).

Increased industrialization reduced the necessity of female participation in all aspects of community life. For many families, survival was no longer dependent upon all family members working. The preferred image of women reverted to that of gentility and purity (Sanger 1958 in Bullough 1974).

While many of the traditions of other cultures influenced the specific gender roles and accompanying characteristics, Richmond-Abbott (1983) describes the societal expectations of males and females in the industrialized United States as particularly and uniquely rigid. In this country, men were and often continue to be thought of as void of emotion, or at least "rational" enough to hide their feelings. Further, a man's status and general worth is characterized by his work, especially according to the amount of money he makes. There is less blurring of gender-specific characteristics, especially emotional ones. The 1980s in this country provide a recent example of the demands placed on individuals based on gender expectations. Accrual of material wealth, power, and influence were understood as the primary measure of status. To obtain these, competitiveness unfettered by emotion was required. These "masculine" characteristics also were required for women who were participants in the climb to success. Perhaps now more than ever the traditional masculine characteristics and the associated roles are valued over feminine characteristics and roles.

The sociological interpretation of the link between gender and role assumption suggests a long history of males assuming roles that have been dominant and public in nature, while females traditionally have assumed roles that have been characterized by less prestige and power and have been less public in nature. From the earliest development of gender role stratification through the growth of the rigid gender roles in early America, gender role stratification endured. As societies defined gender roles, they also came to place differential value on these roles. Males and the roles they assumed came to hold far more prestige than females in their roles.

SCHOOL STRUCTURE AND GENDER

Schools are a powerful tool for socialization in our society. It is important to understand how gender role expectations are reflected in schools and the extent to which they occur. Before the structure of modern schools and their impact on the perpetuation of gender specific roles is examined, it is useful to look briefly at how schools in United States society were formed and what role they played in passing on gender role expectations to children of earlier generations.

Early United States Schools

The first American schools were established in New England. Initiated by the Puritans, their traditional Calvinist beliefs were the basis for what and how things were taught. The all-male church leaders prescribed a curriculum that focused on sufficient reading skills to allow children to read the Bible and maintain the traditional religious and cultural values. All children in these homogeneous communities eventually were able to attend school free. By 1750 most New England communities taxed their residents in order to pay for the schooling. Although communities were required to have schools, attendance was not compulsory (Hill 1967).

Town meetings, presided over by church leaders, became places where all community business was discussed. Because the leaders had a vested interest in the schools, school issues were agenda items at town meetings. Thus the concept of community input into schools, or a school board structure, began. Males constituted the power structure within the communities, and this male dominance extended into the control of the schools. Male dominance of school boards remains the norm today (Clabaugh & Razycki 1990).

In the middle colonies, less homogeneity existed within areas. More religious groups existed; therefore there was a broader array of school philosophies. However, the aspect of male control over schools was present in this region as well (Clabaugh & Razycki 1990).

Community schools were rare in the southern colonies. Sons of wealthy men often went to Europe for their private education. Daughters generally were unschooled altogether except for learning skills considered necessary for their passive and restricted role within the culture. Poorer boys and girls were not schooled at all (Clabaugh & Razycki 1990).

Higher education, modest as it was, was established in both the north and south as a means to further the education of wealthy males and bore the stamp of the dominant religion of the region. Harvard, opened in 1636, was established in order to assure the New England colonies of a sufficient supply of ministers. The charter for William and Mary College in Virginia was obtained not long after, with the same purpose as Harvard (Knight 1941).

It is interesting to note that the hierarchical control of Harvard was, from the beginning, given to a president and a board of trustees. Unlike the system in England, faculty did not govern themselves. Higher education was the exclusive enclave of men. A pattern of male dominance in higher education, both in who participated and who administered, was established and continues to the present in nearly all American higher education institutions (Clabaugh & Razycki 1990).

Although each region was distinctive in the structure of its schooling, one aspect was constant among them: power over the establishment as well as the particulars of schooling were considered masculine enterprises. Male students were much more likely to profit from schooling, and in many situations they were the only participants in the system. Many of these traditions remain today.

Women in Teaching

During the colonial period and into the early years of nationhood, men constituted most of the teaching force, with two exceptions. Some community schools held a short summer term. Women were allowed to teach these brief sessions, in which children were taught the most rudimentary lessons. The other exception was the dame school. Single women, often widows, taught primary education to boys, and less often girls, in the community. These women constituted a small percentage of the teachers in early America (Hoffman 1981).

In regions where teachers were other than ministers, men who were seeking part-time employment often took up teaching as something to do until they could find more lucrative work. The position of teaching was one of very low status and salary. Most are familiar with Washington Irving's portrayal of Ichabod Crane, who has come to embody the stereotypical teacher of the colonial period. He was a laughable, weak, and stupid creature who commanded respect from no one. This caricature of colonial teachers exemplified, in an exaggerated way, the lack of power and prestige teachers held in the society (Hoffman 1981).

The first of the normal schools, academies established to train future teachers, opened as the Lexington Academy in Massachusetts in 1839. Young women began to train as teachers for rural and the growing urban schools. By 1860, women held the majority of teaching positions (Hoffman 1981).

Women came to be employed in substantial numbers as teachers for several reasons. More schools were needed, due to the greatly increased numbers of children in many regions of the country. In addition, with the advent of the industrial revolution, expanded occupational choice for men unfolded. Due to what were considered the "natural" characteristics of women—nurturance, gentleness, and a maternal relationship with children— women became considered natural teachers for younger children (Hoffman 1981). Supporters of women in teaching spoke of the primary school as an extension of the family; therefore, it became socially feasible to allow women this employment opportunity. The growing number of proponents of women as teachers explained their support similarly to Horace Mann:

> Some of the arguments in favor of this change (employing women teachers) have been the greater intensity of the parental

> instinct in the female sex, their natural love of the society of children, and the superior gentleness and forbearance of their dispositions—all of which lead them to mildness rather than severity, to the use of hope rather than of fear as a motive of action, and to the various arts of encouragement rather than to annoyances and compulsion, in their management of the young (Woody 1929, 483, in Weiler 1989).

The gender role of women, which had long restricted most of them within the confines of the family, was in a sense expanded—and in another sense it was not. The view that all women held specific feminine characteristics and were only suited for a limited role in the world remained fairly unchanged, while slightly more opportunity for operating within the limits of those characteristics was provided. The view of women as being distinctly and inherently different from men remained (Weiler 1989).

Women's sexuality continued to be an issue. Because of the concerns surrounding women's sexuality, teachers' lives were limited in social interaction and attainment of power in the larger community, in part due to the need to keep them sexually pure. In accordance with Judeo-Christian teachings, women, once married, were no longer virginal and therefore not pure. Instead they became (albeit unspoken) sexual beings and therefore were no longer appropriate for association with children in the classroom. Women teachers lived under a strict behavior code that kept them away from men. Once married and sexually "contaminated," they were unfit for the classroom (Hoffman 1981).

A final reason for women's entrance into the teaching work force was the desire on the part of society to provide schooling for larger numbers of children and at the same time not have to pay much for that service. Through the efforts of reformers such as Horace Mann, common schools began to be established in many parts of the country. These schools were designed to provide common educational experiences for most of the children within a community. In order to staff the schools inexpensively, women were allowed to take the positions. As they were not considered the equals of men physically, intellectually, or socially, it was accepted that they could be paid considerably less than men (Weiler 1989). This pattern of differentiating pay by gender was in effect from the beginning of established schools until well into the twentieth century.

In his eleventh annual report as secretary of the Massachusetts

Board of Education in 1847, Mann expressed concern about the low level of teachers' salaries and the variation of average salaries among regions. However, concern was not expressed about the differences in salary by gender. This difference was an accepted and acceptable fact.

> Look at the average rate of wages paid to teachers in some of the pattern states of the Union. In Maine it is $15.40 per month to males, and $4.80 to females. In New Hampshire it is $13.50 per month to males, and $5.65 to females. In Vermont it is $12 per month to males, and $4.75 to females . . . Even in Massachusetts it is only $24.71 per month to males, and $8.07 to females (Monroe 1913).

By 1910 salaries had risen, but the gender discrepancy continued. The average monthly salary across the nation was $68.86 for men and $53.40 for women. In order to offset the problem of teachers leaving the job, school districts, particularly in the larger urban areas, began to institute salary schedules after 1900.

> Under the necessity of providing a stimulus for permanency of the teaching corps, a majority of the urban school systems have established graduated salary schedules. These salary schedules provide for minimum salaries for particular grades of service, together with periodic increments to a maximum. These increments are based generally on service alone, although the tendency to condition them upon meritorious service is marked (Monroe 1913).

Salary schedules were generally structured such that a men's schedule and a women's schedule were kept separate. Women earned approximately seventy-two cents for each dollar earned by men (Monroe 1913).

During this time of the feminization of teaching, many who were considered advocates of women in teaching supported the concept of women being paid less than men. For example, Catherine Beecher (1800–1878), a celebrated supporter of improved teacher training for women, used the following point in her argument:

> It is WOMAN who is to come in at this emergency (increased need for teachers) and meet the demand. Woman, whom experience and testing have shown to be the best, as well as the cheapest, guardian and teacher of childhood (in Larkin 1988).

Such a statement is consistent with other perspectives of Beecher's about differentiated gender roles. She was particularly outspoken against the early women's movement, against allowing women to enroll in higher education institutions, and against women's education becoming purely "intellectual" (Goodsell 1931). She firmly believed that women's role was distinct from men's and no blurring of roles was appropriate.

Due in part to the women's movement as well as the beginnings of union and professional association activity in schools, men's and women's differentiated salary schedules were eventually balanced. Nevertheless teaching salaries, as well as the prestige accorded to the position continued to be low compared to other positions in society (Monroe 1913).

As the feminization of teaching progressed, many in society registered concern. From 1875 until 1910, the proportion of male to female teachers steadily dropped. In 1875 men made up 42.2 percent of the teaching force. By 1910, men constituted only 21.1 percent of the teachers in the United States. Among those in authority and policy-making positions in education, this dramatic increase in the number of women in teaching was viewed with concern. Social, economic, and pedagogical problems were cited. The social problem was one of women holding teaching positions for a short period. Upon marrying, they would take their natural positions as wives, then mothers. As new teachers were hired to replace those who left to marry, this process was said to create a continual succession of inexperienced and immature teachers through the classroom (Monroe 1913).

The worst economic dilemma facing administrators and policy makers was how to attract male teachers. As salary schedules became gender neutral (after the middle of this century), the salary levels tended to be lowered to reflect the lower status of women. Few men, of course, were willing to work in an occupation that bore the stamp of low salary, power, and prestige associated with women's work (Monroe 1913).

Controversy brewed over whether women were the pedagogical equals of men, especially for positions in the secondary schools. Could a woman teach chemistry or math as well as a man? Further, what would happen to a child, particularly a boy, who was taught only by women?

The traditional attitude of the enlightened social mind as well as of the intelligent individual mind is to regard with suspicion any educational scheme in which, as is the case in the United States, the great majority of children are never, during their school career, in contact with a man teacher. The theory of democracy would seem to demand a place for the woman as a teacher, but not to the exclusion of the man as a teacher. The equilibrium will be established partly through the recognition of the economic law that governs the proper compensation of sexes engaged in the same social service, and partly through the changes that are taking place in all forms of lower education, whereby emphasis is placed upon training in vocational technique that belongs largely to the industries of men (Monroe 1913).

The feminization of teaching occurred over a very short period of time, roughly 1860–1885. Arguments continued about whether or not this was a positive trend. Nevertheless, women increasingly dominated the teaching ranks by a vast majority. Men did not begin to reenter teaching until after World War II. Not until 1960 did the number of men teaching in high schools equal that of women. Despite male reentry into the profession, it continued to be associated with the gender role of females. The characteristics of the traditional woman, less valued than those of the traditional man, were connected with teaching. The result was low prestige, pay, and power for teachers (Hill 1967).

Another gender-related issue in schools is that of power and control. The hierarchial nature of schools as institutions has tended to place teachers in positions where they have little control over their work. The higher ups, those in school board and administrative positions, establish policy and implement it. Since the days of the Puritan schools in New England, these positions have been occupied almost exclusively by men.

Women in School Administration

Although increasing numbers of women are serving on school boards today, particularly in urban areas, overwhelmingly it is men who dominate these policy-making bodies that control the shape of our schools. Ten percent of school board members were women in 1926 as well as 1956. By 1990 only 33.7 percent were women (American Association of School Administrators 1989–90). The prevailing attitude early in the century regarding women on school boards was illustrated by Elwood Cubberly in 1916:

Those who do not make good school board members are inexperienced men, old men who have retired from business, politicians, saloon keepers, uneducated or ignorant men, men in minor business positions, and women (Callahan, 1967, in Stockard, et al. 1980, 83).

While such attitudes are rarely stated publicly in current society, there continues to exist an attitude that instrumental or masculine characteristics are required for such responsibility (Stockard, et al. 1980).

However, a more equal distribution of women and men on school boards increasingly might become a moot point. A trend noted earlier by Zeigler and Tucker (1979) and more recently by Conley (1991) seems to be gaining momentum; superintendents, site administrators, and teachers are enjoying expanded autonomy in their power and decision making capacities while school boards less often micromanage the schools in their districts. However, the one exception to this generalization is a board's role of hiring the superintendent, who in turn usually has the primary responsibility of hiring other line and staff administrators.

Perhaps more than in any other facet of education, the predominance of men in administrative positions illustrates the issue of gender specific roles. Nationally, men hold virtually all of the superintendent, assistant superintendent, building principal, assistant principal, and central office positions that entail the supervision of other adults. Women who do hold administrative positions in school districts often are found in staff positions, with no real authority. These positions often involve coordinating curricula or providing other support services (Schmuck 1980). Even in elementary schools, where women often comprise the entire teaching staff, the principal is more likely to be a man than a woman. In 1928, women held more administrative positions, usually that of elementary school principal, than at any time before or since (table 2.1). The decline since then has been sure and steady (Hammer & Gerald 1990).

Sources cite slightly varying statistics, but a fairly accurate portrayal of the current percentage of men and women in school leadership positions is given below (table 2.2). These figures can be compared to the overall representation of men and women in teaching positions. Women constitute the bulk of the teaching force but very little of the administrative ranks.

TABLE 2.1
Women in School Administration

Year	Percent
1928	55
1948	41
1958	38
1968	22
1973	20
1984	18

(Educator Opinion Poll, 1984)

TABLE 2.2
Men and Women in School Leadership Positions

	Men	Women
Elementary Teachers	15.5	84.5
Secondary Teachers	50.5	49.5
Superintendents	95	5
Principals	78	12
Elementary Prin.	80	20
Secondary Prin.	96	4

(Fauth, 1984 in Carelli, 1989, p. 337)

Figures from 1990 report that men held 95.2 percent of the superintendencies and 72.3 percent of the principalships nationwide (American Association of School Administrators, 1989–90).

Teaching has come to be seen as a "feminine" occupation accompanied by lower status and salary than comparable "masculine" occupations. However, consistent with the tradition of gender role expectations, males dominate positions of decision making and control in schools.

Curriculum

Many aspects of specific gender roles in education are overt. Men are dominant in positions of policy making and administration, and women occupy most of the service positions, primarily as teachers. A less obvious vehicle of gender role differentiation in schools is curriculum. Despite the legal access for both genders to all curriculum areas provided by Title IX, traditional expectations of gender roles continue to influence who participates in various curricula areas. From the earliest days of schooling to the present, female and males have experienced different curricula, as well as the same curricula, differently. Chapter 3 examines the relationship between curriculum and gender in schools today. However, in order to complete the brief history of gender differentiation in American schools, it is useful to examine the beginnings of males' and females' access to knowledge through curriculum. Because the history in western Europe influenced what took place in the United States, differentiated curriculum development in western Europe will be addressed first.

As was discussed earlier, the concern about the true nature of women dates back at least to the beginnings of ancient Judaism. Were women sweet, pure, and nurturing, or were they sexual temptresses who personified evil? This dilemma continued to concern scholars in Europe during the post-Reformation period. On a more practical level, the issue saw light of day in the discussion of whether women should be educated, and if so, to what extent. The interpretation of women's nature and gender role by people in Western Europe bore heavy influence on what was to happen to females in the United States. The condition of females, especially in England, laid part of the foundation for the quality and quantity of schooling that females received in the American colonies and later in the United States (Stock 1978).

The prevailing perception of European women during the seventeenth century was idealized as what we might think of as the traditional woman. However, some women of that time argued against this interpretation. Among them was Anne Marie von Schurmann, of Holland. In her published work *On the Famous Question, Whether it is Necessary for Women to be Learned* (1638), she contended that women were considered inferior to men primarily due to their lack of opportunity for education comparable to that of men. She argued that confining women to domestic life was based strictly on custom, not on innate characteristics that determined women were better suited to this life. A handful of other women from western European countries echoed her sentiments in their writings (Stock 1978). Their concerns went unheard, except in scholarly circles where the debate about women's nature continued. As a result, the majority of females of that day received no formal schooling.

During the seventeenth and eighteenth centuries, small numbers of upper class females were educated in girls' schools or more commonly in convents. There was little consistency of curriculum among these schools, mostly because there was essentially no consensus about what girls should learn. At best, the curriculum offered a sampling of the "womanly" arts: needle work, art work, preparing banquets, making ointments, and cooking (Stock 1978). The rare woman who obtained an education approximating that of a man did so on her own, not through any organized school.

By the late eighteenth century, some females went to schools. However, females who received an education did so according to a curriculum that was conceived of as meeting their needs and intellectual abilities. Their schooling also remained separate from males. In 1779–1789, the Comtesse de Miremont wrote a seven-volume tract, with the approval of the French crown, on the appropriate education for girls. She wrote:

> Girls' training must be distinct from boys'. Women were not destined to learn anything in depth. The study of religion and the accomplishments was to enrich the three Rs, grammar, geography, history, and natural science. Women should never appear learned, but should know enough to understand everything, be bored with nothing, make an astute comment, and enjoy the knowledge of others (Stock 1978, 111).

Her work was well received in France. The writings of Madame Puisieux, *Counsels to a Friend* (1775), were of a similar vein. Her work was translated into English and circulated in England, and reinforced the practice there of restricting women's education.

A challenge to separate and unequal education for women came with the popular writings of John Locke. Locke maintained that the human mind was a blank slate at birth, the idea of *tabla rasa*. The human grew and learned from the impressions received during life. The political interpretation was that all people could become equal given the same education. These important political interpretations tended to be considered by leaders of the day along class lines rather than gender. The idea of women receiving an education equal to that of men was virtually ignored. Even in post-revolution France, where plans were developed for primary education that was to bear the stamp of equality, the most liberal thinkers stipulated that education for girls should continue to be separate and designed to prepare them for domestic life (Stock 1978).

The nineteenth century brought industrialization, initially in England. Increased urbanization was a product of this change. In order to combat many of the problems caused by rapid urbanization, such as crime, child abandonment, and prostitution, as well as to teach the skills associated with the higher technology, universal education gradually developed. Both boys and girls began to profit from free and compulsory primary education over the century. Particularly within the working class, boys and girls tended to receive their primary education together. The education of upper class females in relationship to upper class males was less equalized. These women generally remained in the home and became the model of the Victorian housewife (Stock 1978).

From the seventeenth to the nineteenth centuries, the traditions of rigid gender roles of western Europe confined women to no formal education at worst, and limited gender role-specific education at best. Although there were some differences in the United States, these western European traditions heavily influenced the educational opportunities of women in the United States as it developed.

As discussed earlier in this chapter, some of the earliest primary schools in this country were the dame schools that operated during the eighteenth century in which generally the basics of an education were taught to both boys and girls, although the specifics of the curriculum were usually determined by the knowledge base of the teacher. Teachers were either men teaching temporarily or unmarried women who needed to earn an independent living. The subjects included reading, writing, and learning numbers for children ages four through seven. Needle work was included exclusively as a girl's subject. The purpose of the dame schools was to prepare the boys to go on to the town schools, where girls were usually denied admission. Because attendance often was not compulsory, boys attended more regularly than girls. If education was given priority in a family, the opportunity for it often was restricted to boys (Hoffman 1981).

By the middle of the nineteenth century, middle class children had the opportunity to attend boys' or girls' boarding schools. The curriculum of the girls' schools reflected the needs of girls who would leave school to enter domestic life as wives (Hoffman 1981).

Toward the end of the nineteenth century, the influx of immigrants to the United States were perceived to be creating unprecedented urban problems, particularly on the East Coast. In order to foster the Americanization of the various ethnic groups, to cut down on juvenile crime, and to solve social and economic problems, educators began to consider reform efforts in the schools (Hoffman 1981).

In 1918, the National Education Association's Commission on the Reorganization of Secondary Education released a report recommending that high schools be created that would offer curriculum tracks leading to business, commercial, industrial, domestic, and college options for students. The idea was to steer young people toward marketable skills early on in their schooling. The curricular offerings within the tracks were intentionally narrow in order to focus on the skills needed (Stevens & Woods 1987).

This tracking system, which formally remained intact in many large high schools across the country until a 1967 Supreme Court decision rendered tracking unconstitutional (*Hobson v. Hansen*, 1967), had the effect of segregating students by ethnicity, class, and gender. The problem of substantial over-representation of one gender in a curricular area was pronounced. Boys dominated tracks that trained them for a wide array of work options. Girls were prepared within the "domestic" or clerical tracks or for the fields of teaching or nursing. The decreasing number of male teachers were found teaching in the "male" tracks. Women taught in the "female" tracks and were in the "male" track classrooms when male teachers were unavailable. As these curricular tracks became more entrenched in the high schools, it was hoped that more men could be attracted to teach in order to prepare boys better than women could (Monroe 1913).

As in Europe, women's education in the United States was of a lower quality than that of men. In coeducational schools, the curriculum was gender specific, with female students at best experiencing a watered-down version of the male curriculum. More often they had a totally different curriculum, which focused on preparing them for domestic life. The advent of high schools brought curriculum tracks that prevented females from being trained in skills equal to or comparable to that of males (Hoffman 1981).

Today, due to Title IX and other legislation, gender differentiated curriculum, at least on the face of it, no longer exists. Females are not formally or overtly placed in one curricular track while males pursue other knowledge. Yet it is clear from the research that substantial separation by gender in some curricular areas continues to exist in our schools. In understanding how these divisions by gender are perpetuated, it is useful to examine how, even today, we as parents and teachers continue to socialize our children according to gender roles that are very similar to the roles that evolved early in United States' society.

IMPLICATIONS OF GENDER ROLES TODAY

It is important that teachers understand where and how people learn gender roles so they can address the negative effects of these roles in their classrooms. The gender role expectations within which most adults in our society continue to operate are not determined at birth. Boys and girls are not born with a clear understanding that they should behave in particular ways in order to achieve acceptance within society. This is learned behavior, and the learning begins at birth. A number of factors contribute to this learning process.

Two powerful sources of this knowledge acquisition are the parents and the schools. Many children spend their time at home and in school, hearing direct as well as indirect messages about what is appropriate for them based on their gender. Another influencing factor is the media, particularly television. The research regarding children's television viewing suggests that it helps young people learn about gender-appropriate choices in behavior, clothes, and toys.

Early Childhood Messages From Parents and Preschool Teachers

Research suggests that gender role socialization begins with the earliest interactions between parents and their newborns. Male babies are dressed in blue and female babies in pink. In addition to this superficial differentiation, there are more important differences in treatment.

Parents tend to interact differently with girl and boy infants both in physical as well as verbal ways. Maccoby and Jacklin (1974) found that parents tended to talk to female babies more often than male babies. On the other hand, boys were found to be held more often and in general interacted with more than girls. One possible explanation for parents' reactions is that girl and boy infants actually behave differently and therefore stimulate their parents to act in these differentiated ways (Richmond-Abbott 1983). However, the idea of biological differences in infant behavior is insufficiently supported and has not been investigated to the extent that the issue of parental expectation based on the child's gender has been examined.

A number of studies have been conducted that examine people's gender related expectations. In these studies subjects, usually parents, interact with young children and assume that the children are a particular gender. Some of the children are dressed in traditional gender-appropriate clothing, while others are dressed in clothes of the opposite gender. These types of studies nearly always result in similar findings: that people, even young children themselves when they are the subjects, react to infants and toddlers based on stereotypic notions of the gender they perceive the infants or toddlers to be (see for example Rubin, Provenzano, & Luria 1974; Smith & Lloyd 1978). "He's a tough little guy," or, "Isn't she quiet and sweet?" are examples of typical comments, even when the observer has misidentified the gender of the child. In addition, children thought to be boys tend to be played with in a more rough-house manner, while those thought to be girls are played with in gentler ways. The tone of voice used in interacting with the children differs as well. Children thought to be boys are spoken to in louder voices while quieter voices, are used with children thought to be girls. In studies where parents have been observed playing and interacting with their own children, the same gender differentiation has been found (Maccoby & Jacklin 1974).

By the time children are four years old, they have well conceived notions of their gender identity and gender-role expectations (Thorne 1986). Gender role expectations and gender identity become intertwined, although the former is artificially imposed through society while the latter is biological. At about this age increasing numbers of children move into preschools, where further reinforcement for learning gender roles is provided by preschool teachers.

In a number of studies preschool teachers have been observed to determine whether their interactions with children are gender differentiated (e.g., Serbin et al. 1973 & Fagot 1978). Overwhelmingly, the research suggests they are. As is the case with parents, preschool teachers seem to interact with toddlers and children in gender specific ways. Preschool teachers interact with girls more gently and boys in a more robust way; teachers' voices tend to be louder and more directive with boys. Further, boys are disciplined for behaviors that often are ignored in girls.

Preschool teachers suggest toys and other kinds of play for children based on their gender. Girls are directed to quieter play such as coloring, the dress-up area, or dolls, and boys are encouraged toward play that requires more activity such as block building or "combat." Preschools are often places where little is done to expand the concept of gender roles for children. Despite the fact that the preschool is a logical place for children to begin to learn, through their play, that their horizons need not be limited, they generally emerge on their way to kindergarten with rigid gender role expectations of themselves and others intact (e.g., Serbin et al. 1973; Cherry 1975; Serbin & O'Leary 1975; & Fagot 1978).

Television and Gender Roles

It is an understatement that children watch a great deal of television. It is estimated that children in the United States in grades kindergarten through six watch from ten to twenty-five hours per week. What these figures mean in relationship to other activities in which young people might be involved is that more time is given to TV watching than reading, listening to the radio, and watching movies. By the time a person is sixteen, she or he has seen fifteen thousand hours of TV compared to eleven thousand hours spent in classrooms (Richmond-Abbott 1983). Television is a large part of the lives of young people. How are gender roles portrayed in television, and what part does television play in helping to shape gender roles in young viewers?

An early study, published in 1974, examined the portrayal of stereotyped images of males and females in television. The findings reported that in general, television programs at the time illustrated a distorted view of life. Overwhelmingly, the prime-time programs had male principal characters, many who were engaged in violence as a way of life. Women were in subservient roles or as sex objects and often were the victims of violence (Women on Words & Images 1975).

Tuchman (1978) studied prime-time commercials for stereotypic images of females and males. She found that nearly all commercials used male narrators, even when the product was being marketed to women. Additionally, she found that three-fourths of all commercials using women were for products for the kitchen or bathroom, showing women engaged in cooking or cleaning. Men were most likely to appear in a business situation or outdoors.

Although some television programs produced for adult viewing in the 1990s provide exceptions (e.g., "Murphy Brown," which played upon the 1992 presidential campaign regarding the definition of family values), recent research indicates that not much has changed since the middle 1970s, particularly in children's television. After examining television programming for evidence of stereotyping during the past fifteen years, Signorielli (1989) reports that ". . .Sex roles images, over the past 10–15 years, have been quite stable, traditional, conventional, and supportive of the status quo" (in Comstock & Paik 1991, 159).

Television generally provides an inaccurate view of men's, women's, girls', and boys' lives. In a sense, many of us watch certain programs because of this distortion; the program may provide fantasy or at least a distraction from real-life concerns. However, research suggests, although modestly, that when children watch television their beliefs about gender roles may be affected (Comstock & Paik 1991).

Considerable research has been conducted over the years that examines young viewers' reactions to the gender of main characters as well as the impact of stereotypic programming on the children's gender-role perceptions. For example, Ruble, Balaban, and Cooper (1981) reported that of four-, five-, and six-year-old children, the five- and six-year-olds preferred not to play with a toy when they saw it being displayed in a commercial featuring a child of the other gender. (The four-year-olds of the sample were considered too young to be sufficiently developmentally mature to distinguish between genders and their stereotypically appropriate roles). In a sample of the research conducted with an older group of viewers, Frueh and McGhee (1975) and McGhee and Frueh (1980) studied children in kindergarten, second, fourth, and sixth grades. Their findings indicated that there was a positive relationship between the amount of television viewed and the degree of stereotypic belief about gender roles; the more television the child saw, the more stereotypic his or her views were. The researchers also reported that the amount of stereotyping tended to increase with the age of the viewer if the person was a heavy viewer, while the amount of stereotyping decreased for those who were lighter viewers (in Comstock & Paik 1991).

Some research has been conducted that analyzes teenagers' television viewing and gender role perceptions. Williams (1986) conducted a longitudinal study of 430 sixth and ninth graders to examine the influence of television on gender stereotypes as television programming was introduced into their community. The findings suggested that after two years of watching beauty commercials, girls ages sixteen and eighteen were more likely to consider being popular with males and having beauty characteristics more important than were girls who had not seen the commercials.

To summarize the research in this area, television does seem to have an effect on the gender role perceptions of young viewers. In general, those who hold more traditional views of these roles tend to find them reinforced through television programs. Following their review of the literature on this subject, Comstock & Paik (1991) suggest the following:

> . . . the findings attest to very modest but positive associations between television exposure and the holding of stereotypic beliefs by children and teenagers of both sexes. Television viewing for young persons is a highly conventional use of time, and we would not be surprised to find that those who view more than average are more conventional than average in outlook (Comstock & Paik 1991, 175).

> We do conclude, however, that television certainly reinforces and thus contributes to conventional beliefs. Programming is typically stereotypic and generally favors male ascendancy; males appear more frequently, more often exert authority, . . . and occupations are linked to gender both in kind and by status (Comstock & Paik 1991, 176).

Television, to which many children and teenagers devote more time than to homework and other activities combined, helps reinforce a traditional view of gender roles for both males and females. It is one more aspect of society that poses a challenge for teachers in their attempts to expand their students' ideas about gender roles and to increase their students' understanding of their own potential as well as that of people of the other gender.

Toys and Gender

One of the principal ways children are socialized is through play facilitated by toys. Both at home and in preschool, toy selection is an interesting indicator of learned gender role. Parents tend early on to select toys for their boys that emphasize activity and creativity, such as materials that require building or making something from scratch. Toys for girls often are cuddly and soft and require little activity. They also usually take the form of beings—dolls or stuffed animals. The girl spends time interacting with the toy and developing a relationship. She begins her nurturing training while the boy begins his building and creative activity. In elementary school, boys are likely to receive sports-related toys that require activity and play with a number of other children. The "sports" equipment girls are most likely to have are jacks, jump ropes, or other games played in twos, threes, or alone. As children become old enough to select their own toys, their choices tend to mirror those of the adults who have been selecting for them. The result is that they often prefer toys that are associated with their gender role (Richmond-Abbott 1983).

The issue of toy preference is aided by the marketing practices of toy stores. Toy stores tend to be organized according to girl aisles and boy aisles. (You can conduct your own investigation of this point easily enough. Simply examine an advertisement supplement for a toy store or walk down the aisles of one. You will find that toys are separated into girls' toys and boys' toys. You will find that it is very difficult to find gender neutral toys.) While neither girl toys nor boy toys may be detrimental in and of themselves, the problem is that one gender rarely benefits from the toys that are perceived to be the exclusive domain of the other gender. The child's full range of interests may not be developed because the toy that would aid in that development fits within the expectations of the other gender.

The Stereotyped Boy and Girl

From the earliest age, children learn gender role expectations from parents and other important adults. Even though increasing numbers of women as well as some men hold non-traditional roles today, children often continue to be taught, directly or indirectly, traditional and rigid gender-specific role expectations. Preschool teachers tend to reinforce this learning through behaviors toward and expectations of children that are usually unconscious but nonetheless to the point. As children move into the more formal setting of elementary schools, this reinforcement continues.

As stated earlier, the research strongly suggests that from infancy through early childhood males and females are treated very differently by parents and preschool teachers. As children enter formal schooling, gender role expectations solidify. Chapters 3, 4, and 5 examine curriculum, methods, and teacher-initiated interactions as agents of gender-biased teaching. However, before considering these categories it is useful to gather a general sense of how specific gender-role expectations and the associated stereotypes affect male and female students differently in school.

Nearly everyone can describe the stereotypic attributes of the male student. He is smart, if a bit overactive, especially during his younger years. He is creative and tends to excel in math and science. His passion is team sports, and he is a leader. His affective traits tend to be toughness, competitiveness, independence, and assertiveness or aggressiveness. Demonstration of emotion, particularly of fear or sadness, is not part of his personality. This is especially true as he grows older. These characteristics will make the boy into the successful man. His success will be judged by his ability to achieve, in terms of money and status, in the workplace. The two primary means of instilling these characteristics in male students in our schools are pressure to achieve in the classroom, especially in later schooling, and sports (Sadker and Sadker 1982).

On average, boys begin school at a disadvantage when compared with girls. Developmentally, they are not as mature as their female counterparts during the earliest grades. They also have been socialized differently. While many of the girls have been engaged in activities that are fairly quiet and within small groups or alone, boys often have been active and loud within larger groups. Once in school, boys discover that boisterous behaviors are not appropriate in the classroom. By a large margin they are disciplined more regularly than girls and often have more difficulty staying on task. While boys remain the group most often disciplined until the end of high school (usually a small percentage of repeat offenders), the majority of boys learn the appropriate behaviors and act accordingly. Most begin to apply themselves as students (Sadker, Sadker, & Klein 1991).

Sports in schools have long provided a vehicle for the development of team player skills, competition, and channeled aggression for boys. To excel at sports is considered by many male students to be more important than to excel in academics (Coleman 1960, in David & Brannon 1976). There is tremendous status connected with playing boys' team sports in middle and high school, and this status has a way of extending into the adult workplace.

The sports arena is seen as a microcosm of society. Those athletic gladiators who find victory and glory running between
third base and home plate seem destined to win similar contests
in later years in the corporate board room or on the sales force
of multinational corporations. For the star athlete is competitive, strong, skilled, and a winner. It is a small jump from success on the athletic field to winning at work (Sadker and Sadker
1982, 232).

For boys who are able to become the football captain or the
class president there are great rewards. They are popular with
their peers and adults alike, and they often succeed as adults.
However, most boys do not attain this stereotypic ideal. For boys
whose interests and talents lie in other directions, or for those
who simply are not big enough or tough enough, the traditional
system of rewards for boys does not apply. What paths do these
boys, who are the majority, take in school? They may choose to
ignore the gender expectations of them and operate outside of the
mainstream, or they may spend their years in school attempting
to live up to expectations in the sports or academic arena that
they can never hope to achieve. Either choice can be frustrating at
best or damaging at worst.

Even for men who have succeeded in learning the skills of
competition and winning at all costs, there can be severe consequences, especially later in life. As the man has been attempting to
achieve in the workplace, he is likely to have spent less time than
his wife parenting their children, contributing to work in the
home, or developing a sense of himself apart from his work. He is
less able to express his emotions than a female. Ultimately, he is
more likely to die earlier than a comparably aged woman and
more likely to be the victim of an accident or suicide than a
woman (Sadker and Sadker 1982). If the man has achieved in
emulating the masculine stereotypic ideal, he also may have succeeded in ignoring a great part of his personhood and has missed
developing much of his potential.

The stereotypic concept of girls tends to be the polar opposite
of boys. The girl is a good student, which is to say she is obedient
and stays on task. Feminine curricular areas tend to be considered
language arts, social sciences, and home arts, although toward the
end of high school females are not expected to excel in these areas
(except home economics) as a group over males. The girl may be a
leader within a traditionally feminine arena, but generally not a

leader of the entire group of students. As she goes through the grades she increasingly defers to male students in the classroom academically (Sadker and Sadker 1982).

Despite girls' developmental advantage over boys at the beginning of school, their "appropriate" school behaviors, and their better grades, they lose their advantage over time. For example, throughout elementary school girls report that they do not particularly think of math as being a male domain. However, during the middle-school years, this perception changes. Girls see math as a male dominion. They do not feel as competent in math as they feel boys are (Fennema & Meyer 1989).

Girls tend to take fewer risks academically as well as behaviorally and are much less likely to be seen as leaders. To take on the leadership roles, especially later in high school, would mean a display of assertiveness and competitiveness, which conflict with the expectation of more passivity from the girls (Sadker and Sadker 1982).

Increasing numbers of girls compete in sports organized by the school, and often the sports are played by teams. The similarity to boys' sports ends there. While popularity may be a reward for the girl who excels on a team, her status does not approach that of the male sports hero. Indeed, if the girl is too competitive or aggressive, her femininity might be questioned. Generally, the most common avenue for popularity for a girl with her peers, and with many adults, is still through her relationship with a popular boy. Her achievements are secondary to his, and her status is accrued through his (Carelli 1988).

Girls wear their emotions on their sleeves. Further, the emotions they display are often considered signs of their weakness. Tears are not controlled as they are in boys, evidencing less toughness and more vulnerability. The inability to control their emotions is an indicator that they are less capable of taking on positions that call for more strength and stability (Sadker 1982).

Many girls who assume the traditional gender characteristics find their inability to participate in school on an equal footing with the boys extremely frustrating. However, they may choose to define themselves along fairly traditional lines, because to do otherwise is fraught with too many risks. For the girls who are increasingly choosing to buck tradition within the school structure, there may be few rewards. Although they may achieve in non-traditional academic areas or excel at a sport, the rewards for these activities tend to go to boys rather than girls. Girls for whom the traditional characteristics fit their talents and interests may find themselves unable to find well-paid or high-status work as adults. Within society, feminine characteristics are valued far less than masculine traits. Corresponding to the lower value is lower pay for work associated with feminine traits (Carelli 1988).

Bem's (1975) work with the notion of androgyny suggests that people, especially females, feel better about themselves when they consider their identity to be based on a mixture of masculine and feminine traits. It is not surprising that females feel they benefit more from this combination than males, considering the value placed on traits by the larger society—better to be an independent woman than a dependent man.

In order to reap the greatest tangible rewards in terms of prestige and power, in the short run at least, it behooves a person to adhere fairly closely to traditional gender characteristics and gender role expectations. Our schools continue to shape students according to an established norm, whereby individual potential, regardless of gender, may not be realized.

SUMMARY

A number of forces have helped shape the common understanding of female and male roles and their societal value. Evidence exists that suggests the oldest societies functioned with specific gender roles for its members. As technology advanced cultures continued to restrict females to "feminine work," which tended to be within the home and family structure, and to restrict males to more public roles in commerce, government, and warfare. Women's lives and their contributions passed quietly and undocumented, while men's positions tended to be public, documented, and more highly valued.

Formal religions have further reinforced the separation of the genders, with males in positions of power and females in subservient roles. By the early 1990s, some Christian groups, most notably the Catholic church, became engaged in arguments about women's role in the church, with no resolution to date. While a number of Protestant groups have ordained increasing numbers of women as ministers and priests, the world's largest religions continue to deny women full participation in the workings of the religious institutions.

Finally, the early cultural development of the United States, principally stemming from Europe but gradually taking on a shape of its own, established a strong tradition of gender-role differentiation. This was in terms of both the minutia of daily life as well as the value and power of those maintaining masculine or feminine roles in life.

Schools are a powerful socialization tool in society, and they play a large role in influencing young people in their interpretation of gender role expectations. Schools provide a clear if not directly articulated message; men administer, direct, and manage, while women for the most part teach. Gender roles for adults in schools still tend to follow the construct of the traditional home, where men are acknowledged as the ones in charge while the women provide the care. As boys and girls make their way through the schooling system, this message is not lost on them.

Although today individuals of each gender are often engaged in occupations that in the past were off limits in a very real sense, the evidence of this gender role crossover, at least in terms of occupations, does not seem to be appreciably changing our unconscious attitudes about gender roles. The institution of the schools plays a major role in perpetuating limited opportunities for both genders due to an unyielding concept of what is appropriate for each gender.

A large part of the dilemma in gender bias is that the actions that create it tend to be unconscious and unintentional. Teachers, for example, would rarely say or even articulate to themselves that they intend to work in a biased fashion. Yet gender bias in classrooms is rampant. The subtlety of gender bias makes the issue all the more insidious and difficult to counter. Porter (1988) theorizes that the power of gender bias (as well as bias affecting other groups) emanates from institutional bias. In other words, the structure, rather than the actions of all the individuals, promotes biased treatment of a group or groups (Carelli 1988).

> The institutional model asserts that control over the distribution of resources is a means to maintain the status quo and control outgroup behavior. The ingroup holds control over institutional resource distribution by holding the positions that set informal and formal policy and procedures and make decisions. Outgroups are given limited access to resources and no effective control within the institutional context (1988, 361).

In the case of gender bias, the ingroup that maintains control over the resources is male dominated, while the outgroup is made up of female teachers and female students. This imbalance in resource distribution is acceptable to both groups because it has always been that way; therefore nothing appears to be amiss. By way of example, Porter (1988) uses the societal problem of poverty. Although it is acknowledged as a problem, the solution to the dilemma of poverty is perceived to lay with the impoverished. Rather than consider a more equitable distribution of resources as an answer, it is a general societal inclination to expect the poor person to "just do something" and fix her or his situation accordingly. In an analogous example of gender bias, we expect the female to take on male characteristics in order to be more a part of the ingroup and thus be more deserving of resources.

Implications

This analysis of gender bias is a structural interpretation, that is, it is founded on an interpretation of bias as an integral part of the structure of institutions and therefore is a systemic problem. According to this interpretation, bias is imbedded in the institutions that touch our lives daily (Porter, 1988).

Gender role expectations have a long historical standing in our culture. These expectations are taught to children early by parents and preschool teachers, then they are strongly reinforced by the structure of the schools children attend. The positions men and women typically hold in schools inform students in a subtle way about gender roles. While schooling in general may be considered by society to be feminine, within the occupation of education, the organizational structure of schools reflects that men typically hold the positions of power and higher prestige, while women more often than men provide the daily teaching. This gender differentiation of roles may be one of the more powerful and subtle means of conveying gender-related expectations in the schools to children.

Another vehicle of gender role differentiation in schools is curriculum. A longstanding tradition from western Europe, later transplanted in part in the United States, established a foundation for gender differentiated curricula. Despite laws providing access to all areas of the curriculum for both genders, boys as a group still tend to dominate certain areas, most notably higher-level math and science classes, which lead the way to occupations that hold higher societal prestige and pay higher salaries than fields that do not require these courses. While representation of both genders is broadening across the curriculum, occupational choice remains largely gender-related (AAUW Report 1992).

For many readers, this structural interpretation of bias may ring true. Perhaps from your personal experiences, from reflection about the issues, or from a combination of both, you concur with this interpretation as the primary cause of gender bias. Yet the implications of accepting this understanding of the root of the issue may be troublesome to you as you begin to think about ways to integrate gender equity into your teaching. The essential question is how can you as a teacher expect to counter gender bias in any meaningful way if the problem of bias is so pervasive? It is important to recall that within this framework is the notion that the gender bias is generally perpetuated in an unconscious and unintentional manner. Therefore, despite the pervasive nature of bias, because it usually is not intentionally done, attitudes and behaviors can be changed. The first step is for teachers to take on the challenge of creating classrooms that are free of gender bias. While it may be unrealistic to expect to eradicate bias within the structure of the institution overnight, it is quite possible to remove the traces of gender bias in your own classroom and enhance the realization of students' potential regardless of their gender.

The history of the feminization of teaching, the structure of the institution of schools, and the power of gender-specific role expectations of girls and boys are dominant factors in why we continue to differentiate so strongly between the genders in school. Gender bias is a part of everyday life for most students in their classrooms. This need not be the case. Individual teachers can make a difference.

CHAPTER 3

Curriculum

Two important issues regarding the connection between school curriculum and gender are academic subjects and instructional materials. In the first section of this chapter recent research about these topics is examined. In the second section, Judy, Karen, Mary, Fred, and Pam discuss their curriculum delivery and selection of instructional material.

Curriculum generally is defined as the courses of study provided by the school for students. Elementary schools' curricula, in the strictest sense, can be thought of as content areas such as reading, language arts, science, social studies, mathematics, fine arts, and physical education. In the broader sense, activities that occur in a less formal setting but nevertheless are under the supervision of the school, such as recess and lunch, are considered by some to be part of the curriculum. Secondary schools generally offer curricula that provide greater options in academic areas, as well as in fine arts, sports, clubs, and the like. Here, too, activities that have socialization as their primary purpose, such as dances, are sponsored by the school and may be considered part of the curriculum. The curriculum, or the body of knowledge made available to students, is a potential source of sorting by gender. Several pertinent questions arise for teachers concerned about gender equity in their teaching. Are girls and boys more likely to participate in different parts of the curriculum? And within a given curricular area, do girls and boys experience the curriculum differently?

There are several prevailing assumptions about student participation in the curriculum by gender. One assumption suggests that achievement in various areas of the curriculum tends to fall along gender group lines. A second has to do with participation. For example, one might assume, particularly in secondary schools, that girls are found more often in some curricular areas, while boys are more likely to enroll in courses in other curricular areas. A last assumption concerns the belief that attitudes about curriculum areas differ by gender group. In order for teachers to address real gender concerns in their classrooms, it is important to determine which of these assumptions are unfounded and which are correct.

SUBJECTS

Due in large part to the specific nature of gender roles in our society, aspects of curriculum have long been associated with one gender or the other. A historical perspective of curriculum developed for females was provided in chapter 2. This curriculum was designed to help women function within their domestic role, just as the curriculum for males was intended to prepare them for their gender role. From the tradition of separating bodies of knowledge by gender, we have come to think of particular curriculum areas as being "masculine" or "feminine," or areas in which one gender is likely to do better than the others.

The following sections are an examination of the myths and realities of achievement, participation, and attitude by gender associated with reading, math, and science. These subjects were chosen to the exclusion of others for several reasons. First, most of the research regarding gender and achievement has been focused on these areas. Second, our society and schools emphasize competence in these subject areas. And third, as a society we have developed enduring gender stereotypes that are strongly associated with reading, math, and science. Inasmuch as our society tends to consider competence in these subjects essential for successfully competing in the job market, it is important for teachers to consider their own stereotypic attitudes in light of the myths and realities.

Reading

Reading, which is emphasized more than any other skill in early elementary years, has long been regarded as something in which girls are likely to surpass boys in ability and interest. Is this a valid perception, or is it an inaccurate stereotype? The research provides a complex and inconclusive answer.

Maccoby and Jacklin (1974) reviewed numerous studies that examined this issue and found that, generally, females as a group

TABLE 3.1
Reading Scores by Gender

9 years	13 years	17 years
boys — 207.5	boys — 251.8	boys — 286.0
girls — 216.3	girls — 263.0	girls — 293.8

(U.S. Department of Education, 1990).

tended to do better than males in reading after the ages of ten or eleven. They found no significant gender differences prior to age ten. At the time, these findings conflicted with the rather universal belief that girls as a group outperform boys in reading. More recent research suggests that there is still no conclusive support for or against the belief that girls are better readers than boys.

As reported in the AAUW Report (1992), three major surveys of achievement by gender in United States schools provide mixed results for reading scores by gender. The National Assessment of Educational Progress (NAEP) studied nine-, thirteen-, and seventeen-year-olds. Data reported for these students as of 1990 indicated that girls outdistanced boys in reading scores for each age group.

A second study, the National Education Longitudinal Survey (NELS), began studying eighth graders in 1988. Results from this first sample suggest that girls slightly outperform boys (United States Department, 1990). However, a longitudinal study of high-school tenth and twelfth graders, the High School and Beyond Survey (HSB), found that among those sampled, boys performed better in reading measures than girls. Finally, SAT scores, often cited as a critical measure of how well students in the United States perform in school, showed that in 1976, of those scoring higher than 600 points on the verbal section of the exam, 12.75 percent were male and 13.73 percent were female. By 1989, the female advantage had been reversed, with 13.87 percent male and 10.06 percent female students scoring above 600 points.

Research regarding gender differences in reading often uses as the subjects students who are experiencing difficulties in the subject. Some of the more intriguing research suggests that among a number of nations it is only in the United States that boys are referred at a substantially greater rate than girls for help with reading difficulties. This gender disparity does not occur in other countries where programs for reading problems exist. This phenomenon does not necessarily lend support to the notion that boys cannot learn to read as well as girls, but rather that educators may perceive in advance that boys as a group will have more difficulty than girls in reading and are more prepared to identify these problems in boys (Scott, Dwyer, & Lieb-Brilhart 1985).

With such conflicting data, what conclusion should one draw regarding reading achievement and gender? Some researchers suggest caution when interpreting statistics such as those above. Perhaps the greatest problem in assuming that girls are better readers than boys is that the means of assessing reading achievement may not be as encompassing as it should be. Many skills are involved in reading, such as comprehension and vocabulary knowledge. Yet test scores are generally reported as a single value rather than addressed as multiple skills (Scott, Dwyer, & Lieb-Brilhart 1985). It is possible that when reading skills are considered as one ability an inaccurate picture of gender dominance is portrayed.

Other difficulties in considering the research on reading achievement are looking across age and across ability. Some research suggests that at about the age of puberty girls begin to surpass boys in reading ability. However, the data from the SAT scores demonstrate that, of the group taking the exam (almost all are high school students), boys score higher than girls as a group (Scott, Dwyer, & Lieb-Brilhart 1985).

A possible explanation of male dominance on the verbal portion of the SAT may be that male and female students begin to assess their future in different ways, based on an intensified acceptance of rigid gender roles. Boys approach the end of high school perceiving that they must acquire sufficient skills, probably via college, to be able to attain the status of primary wage earner. Girls, on the other hand, are increasingly more hesitant to compete with boys in the academic arena. Female high-school students do not suddenly suffer significant brain cell loss; rather they tend to persist and compete less. Academic dominance becomes the domain of males, even in the area traditionally considered feminine (Carelli 1988).

It is difficult at best to determine whether reading is a subject in which females do better than males. The different data bases report a rang of findings, from female superiority through high school to males obtaining superiority by the end of high school. The question of whether gender difference in achievement is real is somewhat elusive. The myth, however, appears to endure. Partial evidence of the strength of this myth is the regularity with which our culture identifies males much more often than females to be in need of reading help. Inasmuch as we are the only nation that finds far more boys than girls requiring remedial reading, it is clear we do so based on gender expectations and adherence to the myth of female superiority in reading skills.

Participation by gender in reading tends not to be an issue in the schools. Boys and girls alike receive reading instruction throughout elementary school and often in middle schools. Most high schools require four years of English for graduation. Although boys are more likely than girls to be identified for remedial reading help, boys and girls participate in reading activities within the formal curriculum in the same numbers. There is some indication, however, that preference for different types of reading may exist by gender. Some research suggests that boys are much more likely to read nonfiction, while girls spend more time reading fiction. A secondary finding is that boys regard fiction as a female domain (Winfield & Lee 1986).

While it is not clear whether one gender group actually outperforms the other in reading skills across age and grade, there is some evidence that attitudes toward various reading material may be gender specific. The message to teachers with regard to their efforts in gender equity is that reading material must be carefully selected and varied, with an emphasis on both fiction and nonfiction.

Math

Mathematics bears a similar stereotypic tradition to reading, only reversed. Most groups of people with a relationship to a school—parents, teachers, and students—have tended to perceive math as an area in which males are more likely and females are less likely to succeed. While the research results regarding differences by gender in reading seem to raise more questions than answers, the research about achievement and participation by gender in math is more clear-cut. Much research, particularly that done prior to the mid-1970s, reported that males outperformed females in math almost from the beginning of schooling (Aiken 1971). Other studies reported that by early adolescence boys excelled over girls in math (Suydam & Riedesel 1969). In the mid-1970s, researchers began to take into account an important variable that had earlier been neglected. Previous studies tended to compare the math achievement of boys and girls without considering the fact that boys usually took a greater number of and more difficult courses than girls. As a result of not controlling for participation in courses, large gender differences in achievement were reported. In these studies the girls in the samples simply had less exposure to math than boys; therefore they did worse on tests of math knowledge. Some earlier studies that controlled for the amount of math taken by boys and girls reported fewer gender differences (for example, Fennema & Sherman 1977).

Recent research on math achievement by gender seems to indicate that gender differences have lessened substantially and are declining (Hyde & Linn 1986). The math results of the NAEP illustrated that, other than slightly higher scores for boys in measurement and estimation in grades four and eight, there was little gender difference in the assessment of math skills. For older students, SAT results from 1978 to 1988 indicated a decline in gender differences, although they were still significant (Friedman 1989). During this ten-year period the average score of females increased eleven points, while the average of males taking the test increased four points. By 1988, results indicated that males scored an average of 498, while females averaged 455 on the math portion of the SAT. However, one remaining area of gender difference is higher-level math skills. Both NAEP and College Board data indicate that males outscore females on test items that assess higher cognitive skills (AAUW Report 1992).

A last point about math achievement by gender provides some interesting food for thought. Although we tend to consider standardized test scores as the principle indicator of student outcomes, what of teacher-awarded grades? It might surprise you to know that, despite some remaining gender-related differences in test scores that favor boys, girls as a group tend to receive higher grades from their math teachers. This discrepancy seems to have implications for teachers as they consider their stereotypic beliefs about which gender is more capable in the classroom. It also raises some interesting questions about teacher-initiated interactions as they relate to the gender of students. The issues of quality and quantity of interaction as well as the form of praise and criticism by gender are addressed in chapter 5.

In the discussion of the earlier research of math achievement differences by gender, the issue of fewer girls enrolled in math courses through high school was mentioned as a factor that might have skewed research findings. In general, females did not participate in this part of the curriculum as fully as their male counterparts as the research was conducted. Does unequal participation continue today? The answer is a slightly qualified no. Throughout the sequence of math courses in high schools, female participation is very close to male participation, with the exception of calculus. Data reported by the National Science Foundation in 1989 show that between the years 1982 and 1987 the average number of math credits for boys rose from 2.61 to 3.04. The corresponding numbers for females were 2.46 to 2.93, indicating a disparity of only .11 by 1987. The rates of males and females taking calculus in 1987 were 7.6 percent and 4.7 percent respectively. Through nearly the entire math curriculum, differences in participation by gender are negligible. More equal representation in calculus remains a problem, however (AAUW Report 1992).

The fact that boys are more likely than girls to take upper-level math courses may be indicative of an attitudinal differentiation in math by gender. Some research has suggested that females perceive their experiences in math courses and the relevance of math to their future very differently from males. Fennema (in Klein 1985) has identified three aspects of this issue: socialization, attitudinal, and affective factors. Each of these factors is discussed in the following paragraphs.

The lack of modeling, the strength of traditional gender-role expectations, and a set of experiences that tend to prepare females for math less than males are all socialization factors, which shape females differently from males. Girls are less likely to encounter adult females in roles that support an interest in math than they are to encounter males in these roles. Math teachers in secondary schools tend to be male (U.S. Department of Education 1989), fathers are more likely to help with math homework than mothers, especially when daughters are in middle- and high-school grades (Ernest, 1976), and elementary school teachers, who are generally women, report that they are less comfortable in teaching math than male elementary teachers (Aiken 1970). Although there are increasing numbers of women in the work force who are engaged in non-traditional work that might require a substantial math background, the modeling that is most apparent to female students, at home and in school, tends to reinforce the notion of math as a male domain.

With regard to math specifically, studies report a somewhat inconsistent picture of parental and teacher expectations. In general, when expectation differences exist, they do so in favor of male students (Fennema 1985). For example, one study found that parents perceived math as a more difficult subject for daughters than for sons (Parsons, Adler, & Kaczala 1982). Other work has found little or no difference in expectation by gender (for example, Parsons, Kaczala, & Meece 1982). However, even with little current research evidence substantiating a disparity in expectation, it is clear from other research that males receive different amounts and kinds of feedback than females. Feedback for males takes the form of encouragement, praise, criticism, and insistence on producing the correct answer. This "male" feedback tends to be much more encouraging than feedback females often receive. The power of the stronger feedback for males than females may reduce the issue of expectation in its importance in socialization regarding math (Fennema 1985).

Of particular relevance to math is the personality characteristic of independence. Here again gender differences arise. Boys are more likely than girls to be encouraged toward risk taking, rough-and-tumble play, and independence (Richmond-Abbott 1983). Because this quality has been associated with math achievement, there is support for speculation that girls are less prepared to engage in math than boys because they are socialized less well to be independent (Fennema 1985).

In order to continue to pursue an area of study it seems obvious that a student needs to have a mind set that it is possible to accomplish the work or at least that the work is important to do. While these attitudinal factors influence students' achievement in math, the research indicates that the level of confidence in one's ability to do math varies by gender. By the time students enter middle school, girls tend to express less confidence in their ability to do well in math, particularly in the future (for example Fox, Brody, & Tobin 1980 & Sherman 1980). There also appears to be a link between students' confidence level and the courses in which they eventually enroll (Sherman & Fennema 1977 & Sherman 1980). It is not surprising that students who are confident that they can achieve in a particular curricular area are likely to enroll in more courses in that area. Male students express more confidence than female students in math, and we find more of them in the upper-level math courses.

A second attitudinal factor cited by Fennema (1985) is the value students attribute to obtaining math knowledge. Fennema reports that most research in this area consistently suggests that male students are much more likely than female students to consider math important, particularly in connection with careers. Despite the fact that nearly all higher-status and higher-paid careers require some proficiency in math, females continue to consider this content area less important than do males.

Causal attribution, or what a person believes causes success and failure, also influences student attitudes toward math. Research has established that females and males tend to think about the causes of success and failure differently. Males tend to report that their achievement is due to their ability, but that their failure is based on lack of effort. The implications for this interpretation are that male students are more likely to continue to strive for success and work harder next time to avoid repeating a failure. Females, on the other hand, tend to attribute success to an external source, such as a teacher, and associate their failures with their own lack of ability. In the classroom, female students may be less likely to try hard because of the uncertainty of the source of the previous success and feel failure is likely because they lack ability (Fennema & Meyer 1989). This perceived source of failure and helplessness in math class contributes to females' comparative lack of interest in math.

There is evidence that it is not only students who demonstrate gender-specific patterns with regard to causal attribution. In a recent study (Fennema et al. 1990) researchers asked first-grade teachers to identify their two most and least successful math students. These teachers tended to choose boys more often than girls as their most successful math students, even when achievement test scores indicated that in many cases girls achieved at a higher level than boys. In addition, the teachers tended to consider the causes of success and failure of boys and girls in ways similar to students as described above. Boys' success was attributed more to their ability than was girls'. The findings of these two areas of research seem to indicate that students and teachers alike believe that males are the better math students, regardless of hard evidence indicating that there is little difference by gender.

Affective factors, particularly anxiety about math, are a third source (Fennema 1985) of potential gender disparity in who participates in math. Sheila Tobias (1978) coined the term *math anx-*

iety that is popular today. She proposed that females, based on socialization influences that lead to experiences different than those of males, are likely to harbor intense feelings of anxiety or fear while studying math. Because of their negative experiences in the area of math, females fear it so much that they try to avoid it. If unable to avoid it, they are likely to do poorly due to their intense anxiety. While this theory has not been exhaustively tested, in cases where anxiety affects attitudes this result occurs more for females than males (Fennema 1985).

Socialization, attitudinal, and affective factors all appear to play a role in explaining why females participate less in upper-level math courses than their male counterparts. However, none of the factors can be established as the primary cause of the problem, and certain factors may affect individual students more than other factors. Nonetheless, considered as a whole, female students tend to perceive the math curriculum differently than males and ultimately are less likely to pursue a career that calls for advanced training in math.

Science

Math and science are usually thought of as a pair. These subject areas are often taught in a fashion that connects them, if they are not in fact taught together. As we tend to think of math as a male domain, we think of science similarly. And as with the other two areas of curriculum addressed here, it is important to divorce myth from reality with regard to student achievement, participation, and attitude by gender.

Recent research tends to support the assumption that males do better in science than females. NAEP findings over a period from 1978 through 1986 indicate that not only are male test scores higher than female scores but the gender gap appears to be increasing. This is true for younger students ages nine and thirteen, and especially true for seventeen year olds in the sample. The specific areas of male dominance are physics, chemistry, earth science, and space science (AAUW Report 1992). NAEP results also found that 10 percent of the males scored at or above the test's highest levels of cognition, while only 5 percent of the females did so. SAT results from 1988 were similar. However, as was the case in math, despite these significant gender differences on standardized measures females tend to receive classroom grades as high or higher than male students.

Although participation within the general science curriculum shows little gender differentiation, differences are apparent when specific courses are considered. Girls average 3.1 science credits, while boys average only a slightly higher number—3.3—of courses. However, when enrollment in advanced science courses is examined, girls are found more often in advanced biology, while boys enroll more often in physics and advanced chemistry. Figures show a difference of 25.3 percent to 15 percent of males to females taking physics.

Gender differences in attitude toward specific science disciplines are illustrated by the disparate figures of advanced course participation. There are other factors that seem to point to attitudinal differences, as well. The AAUW Report (1992) suggests that girls may be more influenced by encouragement from teachers in their pursuit of science courses and an eventual career in science, and that they may be more affected by negative counseling from school counselors than are boys (Campbell & Metz 1987 in the AAUW Report 1992).

Other factors have been found to appear to affect students' attitudes toward science based on gender. Some studies have found that as early as the third grade boys appear to have had more experience with science activities and equipment than girls, and this experiential disparity widens throughout high school (Reyes & Stanic 1988). By the sixth grade, students begin reporting gender-specific interests in particular areas of science. Boys express interest in physical and earth sciences, while girls are more interested in biology (Bottomley & Ormerod 1981; Clark 1972). Finally, by the time they reach the end of high school girls indicate a much less positive view of science than boys, including their perceptions of their own competence in science as well as their view of themselves in a science-oriented career. Females see themselves as less competent in science and less interested in the field of science as a career choice than males (Reyes & Stanic 1988).

Causal attribution appears to be the same by gender regarding science as it is in math; females are more likely to attribute any success to external causes and failure to their own lack of ability (Reyes & Padilla 1985). In general, females express much less confidence in their ability to perform in the science classroom than males. A final factor affecting females' attitudes toward science may be societal expectations of females in general. The stereotyped image of the scientist in our society is generally at odds with traditional gender expectations for females. The instrumental characteristics of independence, rational thinking, and risk taking conflict with the more expressive traits traditionally attached to females (Curran 1980).

Factors that seem to prohibit many females from succeeding in and pursuing higher-level math and science should be addressed by teachers in their daily practice. Socialization, attitudinal, and affective factors that have been shown to adversely affect females' success and participation in both math and science should be dealt with consciously by teachers as they implement the curriculum in their classes. While the question about gender disparity in reading capabilities remains unanswered in a definitive way, there is no question that the prevailing stereotype of female dominance in this skill area also must be considered. Teachers must provide sufficient support within the classroom such that boys accept reading activities as part of their role, rather than persist in classifying reading as a girls' activity.

INSTRUCTIONAL MATERIALS

One of the primary means of implementing a curriculum is through the use of instructional materials. While some of these materials are chosen for teachers by others, most notably state-approved textbooks chosen by textbook selection committees, many teachers maintain substantial autonomy in the selection of nearly all other materials.

Recent data suggest that students spend at least 90 percent of their learning time in the classroom using some sort of instructional material (Scott & Schau 1985). While textbooks are the items most easily identifiable as instructional materials, other items probably are used as often if not more so. Workbooks, pamphlets, anthologies, encyclopedias, tests, supplementary books, paperbacks, programmed instructional systems, dictionaries, reference books, and classroom periodicals all fall under the heading of instructional materials that are used regularly by teachers (Scott & Schau 1985).

What role do these materials play in the consideration of gender issues in the classroom? As students progress, they learn to read, to compute, to write, and to question and think with the aid of various materials. The illustrations and stories that provide the setting for instructional content send powerful, often subtle messages that the students incorporate into their understanding of life around them and their place in it.

As discussed in chapter 2, children by the age of three have learned to identify their own gender as well as others by gender (Thompson 1975). They also are well on their way to establishing their gender roles. Children in early childhood begin to look at people in terms of characteristics they can classify. Gender is an obvious, easily categorized characteristic. The ability to classify facilitates children's development of conceptions of gender roles—conceptions that may accurately reflect the world or be based on stereotyped notions. While their own life experiences and relationships with people add to their knowledge of what males and females do within their roles, children also are strongly influenced by the depiction of gender roles they receive through instructional materials. This influence may be so powerful that it overrides the direct experience of the child.

Judy reported an occurrence in her classroom that underscores this point. A 4-year-old girl brought a book for Judy to read to the class. The book depicted people who worked in a hospital, and was extremely stereotyped—all doctors were male and all nurses were female. After reading the book to the class, Judy mentioned that people did not need to be a particular gender to do a job. The owner of the book immediately raised her hand and declared that only men could be doctors. Judy pointed out that the girl's mother was a doctor. Undeterred by this fact, the girl steadfastly refused to accept that women also could be physicians, pointing out that the book told her this. This example from Judy's classroom illustrates that instructional materials children encounter can deeply influence their tentative understanding of gender roles and accompanying expectations.

Gender-specific images in instructional materials can have a cumulative effect on students by providing students' gender role expectations. When materials portray inaccurate or stereotypic situations or do not include groups of people in the learning material, students often unconsciously develop distorted perceptions of their own capabilities or the capabilities of others.

Bias in instructional materials has taken a number of forms. While this bias can negatively affect any number of groups of people—ethnic groups, older people, special needs people, or people of particular religious or sexual orientations—for our purposes only the impact on gender will be discussed.

During the late 1960s and 1970s, considerable attention was turned to the perpetuation of gender bias in commercially prepared materials. Groups concerned with women's rights pressed publishers to include females in materials more often and to present females and males in more realistic situations and less stereotyped roles. A great deal of analysis of materials was done in order to highlight the stereotypical nature of most instructional materials that were on the market at the time.

One of the earliest and perhaps most important study undertaken was entitled *Dick and Jane as Victims; Sex Stereotyping in Children's Readers* (1975). The researchers analyzed a large selection of children's readers widely used in United States schools. This work spawned other research that examined materials both for older students and in subjects other than reading (for example, Weitzman & Rizzo 1976; McLeod & Silverman 1973). The findings of this research have been grouped into several categories by Sadker & Sadker (1982).

Invisibility

Females were portrayed in instructional materials at a far lower rate than males. This generalization was true in materials for younger children, such as readers and workbooks, as well as books for older students. For example, literature anthologies used in high schools contained works that were primarily by male authors and with main characters who were usually male. History books rarely mentioned significant women and never spoke of the lives and contributions of ordinary women.

Stereotyping

Most materials contained illustrations or text that showed males and females in situations only according to traditional gender roles. A chemistry text, for example, might show a male chemist working on an experiment in the lab while a female assistant took care of the housekeeping chores. Important scientists pictured throughout the texts were always male, with the occasional exception of Marie Curie. (However, even this isolated example of a woman scientist conforms to gender stereotyping of females. The most frequently used photograph of Curie shows her standing to the side and slightly behind her husband, leaning on him for support. When looking at the picture, the eye is drawn toward

Monsieur Curie. The reader must carefully review the printed material to understand that the picture is meant to highlight Madame Curie.) Children's reading books showed girls in situations where they were afraid, concerned about dirt and their appearance, passive, and unimaginative. Boys were depicted in situations where they took on active, leadership roles and were heroic and strong, never afraid, and creative. Adult women were assigned roles as mother and wife almost exclusively, while men were found occupied in a wide variety of jobs and activities, but rarely in parenting roles.

Unreality

Issues of social significance were often treated briefly and superficially, if at all. For example, when history texts and supplementary books addressed the women's movement, it generally was done in passing rather than treated as a major civil rights concern. The portrayal of males and females only in stereotypic positions distorted the reality that many people do many kinds of work regardless of their gender. Children reading about the "typical" American family (father as the breadwinner, mother as homemaker, and two children, usually a brother and younger sister) as the prototype were placed in the position of questioning the value of their own situation if theirs differed from the families widely depicted in earlier readers.

Fragmentation/Isolation

In response to initial demands of women's rights groups to better represent females in instructional materials, publishers often retained the original text, adding information on females at the end of a section or chapter. For example, in history texts, following the chapter(s) on the Civil War, publishers commonly inserted several pages highlighting Harriet Tubman. The inclusion of this material in this fashion met several needs. It is cheaper to insert pages in a text rather than rewrite the material, and publishers could point to the fact that a significant woman was included in the study of these events in United States history. In fact, the inclusion of Harriet Tubman had the advantage of increasing representation of women and African Americans simultaneously. However, isolating information from the main text trivializes the importance of the material. The message to the reader is that this information is supplementary or superfluous to the major points. Students recognize at some level that the important information is found in the "regular" reading. Highlights or pictorial footnotes are afterthoughts (Sadker & Sadker and Sadker 1982).

The problems of gender bias in instructional materials were the norm in commercially produced texts and other materials published prior to 1980. What changes have occurred since then that address more realistic and equal representation of the genders in materials students work with in schools?

Textbooks and other materials produced recently by the larger publishing houses tend to reflect greater sensitivity toward gender representation than in years past. This is particularly true in children's readers and history texts for older learners; women and men appear in situations that earlier might have been considered non-traditional. Girls are portrayed in situations that were the sole domain of boys in works published prior to 1980. Math and science texts now are more likely to illustrate females as well as males, and math word problems are less male oriented than before. However, some areas remain problematic.

Materials prepared for use in vocational education classes still generally represent the genders in rigid roles. For example, photographs of people engaged in work depict men as the supervisors, carpenters, plumbers, and mechanics. Women still are shown almost exclusively as secretaries, assistants, and observers (Hulme 1988). While supplementary materials exist that help alleviate the gender stereotyped portrayal of workers, most textbooks that are the primary source of instructional material continue to perpetuate the image of rigid gender roles in the work force.

Another problematic aspect of gender representation in materials is centered around the current controversy of inclusion or exclusion of various groups within what might be considered the literature curriculum. Within the realm of English literature, American literature or other such courses, whose works should be presented for student study?

Traditionally, the works included in the literature curriculum have been those written by European or European-descent males. Such works tend to offer males as the main characters. The argument for maintaining the status quo, or continuing to include only those works by male authors of European descent, is the need to preserve the cultural heritage of the United States. The conservative rationale for excluding women's contributions is that their works tend not to be recognized as significant or substantial. In other words, women have not contributed in shaping the culture (Hulme 1988).

For teachers, for whom gender equity is implemented at least in part through instructional materials, the question is not whether to include women's works in the study of European and American literature, but rather which of their works to include and in what proportion to men's works. Those who argue that it is essential for female and male students to read works by both genders insist that, even at the risk of reducing the number of classics presented within the curriculum, important works by female authors and those portraying females as the main characters must be included.

The conflict about whose works best represent great or classical literature continues with issues surrounding gender and cultural groups. The question of whose historical experiences should be presented in instructional materials is an issue for debate as well. However, what appears to be clear from the research is that in order for females to profit more from their experiences with instructional materials they need to see individuals of their gender included more often. As Hulme (1988) points out:

> Reading about successful women has been found to cause girls to have higher expectations of female success, an important component of achievement, as is knowing that there is a historical perspective to achieving women (190).

Females in literature, both as authors and characters, as well as females' role in world and United States history must be part of the curriculum so that both male and female students come away with a clear sense of the value and contributions of both genders.

HOW TEACHERS SELECT THEIR MATERIALS

Careful selection of instructional materials for classroom use is one of the most straightforward aspects of working toward gender equity in teaching. Once the teacher is aware of the history of unequal and distorted representation of the genders in materials, analysis of what is used in the classroom is not difficult. Many major publishing houses now publish guidelines that aid teachers in their review of materials. In general, these guidelines suggest

that teachers check for a balance of male and female figures represented in readings, for both genders illustrated in all occupations,
for both genders represented in historical accounts and literature,
and that the language of the book not perpetuate gender bias (the
use of sexist language is addressed in more detail in chapter 4).

While helpful, these guidelines do not illustrate how teachers
working toward gender equity think about material selection for
their classrooms. The following discussions with the teachers who
provided information for this book give more useful insight into
how they think about materials and which ones they choose. In
each case, I precede the discussion of materials used by a teacher
with an overall discussion of the curriculum within which the
teacher works.

Judy's Preschool Class

As director of the preschool, Judy has more autonomy than most
teachers. She is able to select materials for use with her students.
Every book, toy, or any other item used with the children is chosen with gender equity as a selection criterion. In addition, she is
largely responsible for developing the curriculum for the school.
Because she constructs the curriculum with gender equity in mind,
it is easier for her to implement gender sensitive experiences for
her students through materials that are non-sexist (neutral in their
portrayal of the genders) or anti-sexist (provide heavy emphasis
of both genders in non-traditional activities).

The curriculum of the preschool was developed to give three-,
four-, and five-year-olds developmentally appropriate activities
and experiences that will eventually prepare them for formal
school. This is true for both special-needs and nonspecial-needs
children. Motor skills, language development, and socialization
skills are all emphasized. As with all aspects of her role as a
teacher and according to her interpretation of gender equity, she
thinks of the curriculum within an equal framework. All children
have access to all activities, are treated equally and evenly, and are
verbally encouraged to do all things. As suggested in chapter 1,
Judy refuses to force students into activities in which they do not
choose to participate. This includes boys who will not enter the
home center and girls who will not build with the carpentry
block. However, she establishes a rule early in the year that no
child can exclude another from play for any reason.

Consideration of materials is an important component in Judy's conception of gender equity in her classroom.

> I look at this issue in two parts; one is non-sexism and the other is anti-sexism. The non-sexism piece especially pertains to materials I use; books, puzzles, play characters. For instance, I have interesting male dress-ups as well as interesting female dress-ups. I carefully screen things. When we sing songs, we sing "cowboy" as often as "cowgirl." The "girl down the lane" and "the boy down the lane." I use materials to contradict stereotypes just in terms of visual images, and as starting off points for discussion.

Judy uses materials that she believes are non-sexist and anti-sexist. The former portray the genders in a variety of traditional and non-traditional roles. The latter focus on the genders in non-traditional roles and are used to counter gender stereotyped attitudes.

Within the centers scattered around the classroom, a variety of materials are visible. The reading center holds books that are fairly new and carefully chosen for their lack of gender stereotyping. The traditional fairy tales are not present. Of all the examples of children's literature, Judy finds these are the most gender stereotyped. Cinderella, Snow White, and Sleeping Beauty are examples of stories that cast the male figure as the hero who saves the helpless and abused female heroine. Instead she chooses books that portray males and females in positions that allow both to be empowered and self-sufficient.

During one day of observation, Judy called the children into the reading circle for the daily reading period. That day she chose to read them a story about a child who lived on a ranch and worked with the parents in all the daily activities. The pictures of the story as well as the language subtly obstructed the gender of the main character. During the reading of it, however, several children whispered among themselves about the "cowboy" in the story. The last page of the book identifies the main character as a she, but only once and without over-emphasizing the point. One female student remarked "It was a girl!" Judy said, "That's right," and went on to the next activity.

When asked about other reactions of the students to materials she uses that are either non-sexist or anti-sexist, Judy cited several examples where she is likely to receive far more reaction than she did with the cowgirl story.

If there is a story or song or some activity that is very anti-sexist, there will always be some children who argue that that's just not how it is. Police officer is always the one. I have a book with a female doctor, too. I ask the children, "What do you think her job is?" The first guess is that she's a nurse. So there are always children whose reaction is that's not how it is.

Another thing that came up was around dance. One of our boys goes to dance class. All the other people in the dance class are girls. One of the children said, "You can't be in the dance class, you're a boy." We talked about when we went to the ballet. I said, "Did you see any boy dancers?" They said, "Oh yes, at the Nutcracker, he was a boy. And the rat king was a boy."

The older children (five years old) certainly are aware of what the gender expectation is. We have one little boy who always dresses up in the petticoats and things. Some of the children are very troubled by that. We talk about that this is pretend, you can be anything you want to be. He can even say he is a girl. It's pretend.

Another example is Who's going to be the daddy? Who's going to be the mommy? They say, "Well, he can't be the mommy and she can't be the daddy." Then I turn it around a little, ask if all women are mommies and all men daddies? For some of them it's difficult to disassociate even that gender role. I have to remind them that they may have an aunt or uncle who isn't a mommy or daddy.

Judy selects some materials that are intended to provide a balance of gender representation (non-sexist) and some that are meant to counter gender-stereotyped attitudes by presenting the genders in non-traditional anti-sexist roles. She believes that both types of materials are useful. The non-sexist materials provide subtle and usually unremarked-upon themes of both males and females occupied in a variety of activities. Children see models of both genders doing all types of things. The anti-sexist materials tend to provoke the students to question their attitudes and beliefs about gender roles. As students remark about what a person can or cannot do based on gender, Judy has the opportunity she seeks to create cognitive conflict in the students' thinking. She uses the anti-sexist materials to provide a basis for the children to begin to question themselves about their attitudes.

The home center houses a collection of construction hard hats and flowery sunbonnets. The baby dolls who live there are of Hispanic, Asian, African, and European decent. They are male and female and are anatomically correct (including some with diaper rash). The building centers have blocks and carpentry tools. Both boys and girls are encouraged but not coerced into playing in these centers each day. And after a number of hours of observation, it is clear that some of the girls simply do not want to play with the more traditional "boy" toys nor some of the boys with the "girl" toys.

Consistent with her resistance to propagandizing her students with the "correct" set of gender equity values, Judy does not require rotation among the centers. Instead, she ensures that all materials are either non-sexist or anti-sexist. Because simple provision of materials is not enough to help the students understand that they are not limited by rigid gender roles, she constructs careful dialogues that cause them to ask questions.

Karen's Kindergarten

As a kindergarten teacher in a very large school district (approximately sixty thousand students), Karen has minimal input into the shape of the overall elementary curriculum across the district. However, because she was an original member of the staff that developed the magnet-school program, she has had considerable influence in designing the kindergarten curriculum at the school where she works.

During the beginnings of the magnet program, Karen and the other kindergarten teacher participated in a gender equity program. Funded through federal money, the program's purpose was to interest and train teachers in gender equity in teaching. Karen and her colleague were so interested in gender equity that they subsequently published a book detailing activities and other means of implementing gender equity. Other teachers in the school came to share their enthusiasm, and nearly all began to teach in ways that were sensitive to gender issues. The general curriculum for the school specifically reflected concerns of gender equity.

When asked whether she perceived the same commitment within the faculty toward gender equity today, Karen responded that in the beginning of the magnet program in the school,

> gender equity was the premiere focus, when we really worked diligently. I think it has become a part of all of us to varying degrees. Some people are really on it still. And some have not moved much further than that initial awakening. Some have continued to grow and change on this stuff. Others haven't.

Despite her sense of less than total collegial interest in and support of gender equity, Karen continues to consider the issue of primary importance for her students, and for her it is indeed a passion.

Karen operates with considerable autonomy in designing her own lessons, which meet the broad goals of the school (literacy and creating an understanding of the world as a global community). The activities she chooses for her students often are not the same as those chosen by other kindergarten teachers in the school. In the same vein, the materials she chooses are likely to be unique to her classroom. She talks about the types of materials she uses as well as how she manipulates their content to address gender equity in her teaching.

> I use a lot of books. Many of them are gender stereotyped. And I use folktales a lot, which are very stereotyped. So sometimes I turn them around. I use the same technique with books I read about real kids. I will read once the way it is in the story, and then go back and read it with the other gender in the lead. Then we will talk about that. We do a lot of switching around of the "he" and "she."
>
> I still find in most of the books I use that male characters predominate. Even when we do animal stories, they (the authors) make them male. But those are easy to switch because they're pretty androgynous.
>
> There are books coming out now where you can't really tell the gender of the child in the story. We talk about that. Kids at this age are still really defining the gender of another child by how the child is dressed. Or by the hair. If it's long, it's a girl; if short it's a boy. That has caused some issues in our room with Thomas and Susan.* There were some great debates at the beginning of the year about which was which and who was who. "Would they stay that way if they got their hair different?" It's based on observable characteristics.

(*Thomas's hair was the longest in the class, fashioned in cornrow braids. Susan's hair was cropped very short. She favored jeans, jean jackets, high-tops, and white T-shirts. Until Karen mentioned it, I thought Thomas was a girl and Susan was a boy.)

Karen tends to steer away from commercially packaged materials, other than books. And as she stated, she switches the gender of the main character regularly. While her students are well aware that she is doing this, they usually don't know whether the story originally was written with a boy or a girl as the leading character.

Karen's intention is for the students to see both genders in all activities without the students knowing that the author's intention was to have the main character be a particular gender. They hear of a man as a nurse and a woman as a nurse; a man as a firefighter and a woman as a firefighter. With the gender evenly and simultaneously represented in situations, students are less likely to see the male nurse or the female firefighter as oddities.

As in most kindergartens, the bulk of the instructional materials are concrete and manipulative. As Karen determines which materials to use, she uses freedom from gender stereotyping as one guideline.

> I wouldn't, for example, bring in Barbie dolls and I wouldn't bring in war toys, although there are other reasons for that decision in addition to gender issues. But we do have carpentry tools and household items. I make sure there is equal access to those.

Karen uses her careful selection of materials as a means to address her goals for gender equity in her classroom. Based on her interpretation of the issues through a framework of *equal*, Karen attempts to be certain that the variety of items used in the class represents interests of both genders and that all students receive equal access to and experience with these items.

The centers in the room are similar to those found in any number of kindergartens: a reading center with headphones for tapes in addition to books, a block center, a home center, and the rug area, where the entire class meets to talk and listen to the teacher and among themselves. The reading center contains books carefully selected by Karen with equality in mind. The block center houses many large blocks and is roomy enough for six children to play at a time. And Karen has taken care to supply the home center with baby dolls of various racial/ethnic backgrounds and of both genders. The home center is quite similar in Judy's room, with items that might interest both girls and boys. While at first blush, the center setup appears quite traditional, on closer scrutiny it is clear that materials have been carefully chosen to emphasize high interest and to avoid traditional gender role stereotyping.

Mary's Third Grade

The curriculum of the school in which Mary teaches has been developed over time primarily by the principal in conjunction with teams of teachers from each grade level. The general goals are spelled out, as are those for each content area. Competencies for all aspects of each curricular area are numerous, and each teacher is expected to address these competencies.

There is much more consistency here among teachers across a grade level than is found at Karen's school. Unit lessons tend to be taught at the same time, and major instructional materials used among classrooms are the same. This is intentional, to ensure that students end the year being exposed to instruction that is common across classrooms at each grade level. Although there may be less autonomy in curricular and instructional matters than in other settings, Mary makes a concerted effort to bring materials to her classroom that provide a gender balance to a topic.

> When I choose, it's more by unit than by lesson in terms of gender balance. If I'm using examples of a reading, whether it's students' own work or other readings, then I try to have a gender balance. If there's a real gender difference that is historically based, I will try to show both sides of it. And I think that's true when we do things with other cultures as well. We do some things about African American heritage. There were some cultural differences that were gender based. And at some point I will point that out.

During part of the time her class was observed, the students were engaged in a unit about United States pioneers and non-native American settlement of the West. Because the bulk of commercially produced materials do not include sufficient information about women's experiences, Mary sought out works about and by women to share with the class during the story time following lunch. One particularly engrossing work was a diary by a woman who moved West with her family. As Mary read the diary entries over a period of days, she stopped periodically and discussed with the students how the author's experiences differed from those of her husband, based on the different gender role expectations in the nineteenth century.

Over another period of observation, Mary read to her students an account of a boy's dog-sled racing experience in Alaska. During and after the reading, she updated the listeners about the status of Alaska's Iditarod dog-sled race, which was currently in progress. At the time a man was in the lead, which Mary reported in some detail. She also informed her students about the status of Susan

Butcher, a four-time winner of the race. The message was clear to the students: both men and women could compete in this event.

Students in Mary's class occasionally comment negatively about the inclusion of the feminine perspective, such as in the case of her use of the woman's diary. Because Mary is insistent upon providing such materials and making their value clear to the students; she does not let moans and groans issued by some of the boys go unaddressed.

> Some of them [boys] get pretty hot under the collar, especially if I say something they perceive as inflammatory, as I often do. With the book we're reading about the dog-sled race, there are some different perceptions. The fact that the real race has been led by a woman for the past five years, that's perceived pretty positively by the girls. Not nearly so positively by the boys. But there's a male in the lead right now, so there are things like that they react to.
>
> If there's a lot of real stereotypical things in a book, I point out it's sexist, and I use that word—not constantly; I don't harangue. But if there's a real power difference, especially if it's in the book and gender related, I comment on it. And the kids will say now, "That's sexist." I think they're getting more aware of it.

During the course of a school year, Mary's students produce several plays, which she uses as a vehicle for further enrichment of a unit of study. Mary believes that this use of instructional enrichment can be an area in which gender roles can be expanded, or ignored altogether.

> Even in plays, I don't limit them [the students] by saying that a girl can only be a girl and a boy can only be a boy. I don't say they have to play something else if that's what they want to do. At the end of one unit, we did a play which was a culmination activity. Sam was a girl. He was a sister in the play. Right now, Cathy is a man in the role of John Mansfeld. She wanted to be in a position of power, which it was. I couldn't tell her it wasn't, so she chose to be a man.

Mary works to provide a gender balance with regard to the materials. Male and female experiences and perspectives are presented, and all students are provided the opportunity to see models of their own gender in both historical and current situations. Some students also are comfortable enough within the classroom environment to ignore the constraints of traditional gender roles, as illustrated by the boy and girl who chose parts of the opposite gender in the plays. Mary's commitment to keeping the issue of gender stereotyping alive among the students is designed to enable the boys and girls to broaden their interpretations of what it means to be male and female.

Fred's Middle-School Social Studies Class

The general curriculum in the middle school in which Fred teaches reflects much of the current trend in middle-school curriculum planning. For example, courses are integrated and offered in block periods of two hours. Students take math/science and English/ social studies for four hours daily in alternating nine-week periods. The remainder of their school day is spent in exploratory courses such as music or vocational education classes.

Recently, the teachers and administration chose to make all exploratory courses mandatory for all students. This was in direct response to the previous pattern of student sorting both by culture and gender. The principal in particular strongly believes that, in order to reduce the tendency of girls to steer away from the courses they might perceive to be "masculine" (technology and computers) and boys from those they see as "feminine" (musical theater and art), all students must take all courses. In this way equal access is ensured.

Fred believes that a primary means of working toward gender equity is through integrating gender issues into the social studies curriculum. As one of the architects of the eighth-grade curriculum, Fred had considerable input into how this is to be done. Presenting perspectives from minority groups within society was considered an important issue and is represented as separate, as well as integrated material within the course of study.

> From the beginning, we've been teaching about this. In fact, in the eighth-grade curriculum the primary emphasis has been on a minority point of view. Gender is a part of that. One thing I can say about this district is that they've always been real supportive about access to materials and of teaching about different points of view.

As Fred teaches principles of democracy and the study of United States government, he carefully chooses material that facilitates teaching about groups other than the white, male majority.

In history and government there's more available now, in terms of lessons, about the role of women. Whereas when I started twelve years ago, it wasn't as available. Now, it's a matter of fitting it in and making sure it's covered. I make a conscientious effort.

During one period of observation in Fred's class, students were engaged in studying the United States Constitution. The assignment for the day was to design a constitution that would directly address equity issues not reflected in the existing document. The material he chose for this discussion was a handout that analyzed the Constitution in terms of equity issues. For example, headings included "Who could Vote" and "Who could be Elected to Office." A discussion of groups excluded from participation in the original form of government ensued. Fred suggested to the group that the history of women participating in government was different from men's. While his teaching style does not lend itself to impassioned lectures about social injustice, his nudge toward student reflection about inclusion and exclusion laid the foundation for questions and discussion about gender issues.

Pam's High-School Health Class

The comprehensive high school in which Pam teaches reflects curricula commonly found in high schools. Courses in the content areas required for high school graduation as well as courses in areas that are offered for special-needs students and academically advanced students are available, along with an array of electives. The curricular goal of the school is to offer students the courses they need in order to pursue life after high school, in the tradition of the comprehensive high school.

As with most schools offering a choice among electives or advanced courses, substantial sorting of students by gender takes place. However, in the case of the course Pam teaches, all students must pass it in order to graduate. Health is a nine-week course that is taken most often in the sophomore year.

The content for the course is prescribed, and Pam has had little input into it. She also has no authority to order instructional materials for the course. But within the larger context of a bureaucratic and top-down school system, Pam does have some control over the topics she chooses for study that fall under the broader headings. These headings include drug abuse, venereal disease, mental health, and health careers.

As part of the mental health topic, Pam includes discussions of gender issues.

> We start with mental health and finish with sex education. We talk about gender role stereotypes and how that fits in with mental health. We also talk about who's more sexual, males or females, and we talk about double standards.

Another instance of Pam's adaptation of the curriculum to bring to light gender-related issues is her insistence that concerns specific to one gender be studied by all the students. Anorexia and steroid use in weight training are given equal time and are studied by everyone. However, students often grumble about the irrelevance they perceive some of these topics to their own lives.

> When they react, and they all do, I say, "Well, it may pertain to someone else you know." Especially about sexual assault. The guys come in and they want to know about rape. I say "This includes molestation, too." I give them a newspaper article about a high-school guy who was raped recently at another high school in town.

Although Pam's autonomy is much more limited than that of the other teachers discussed, especially with regard to curriculum development and instructional material selection, she has fashioned a way to incorporate important gender-related issues into the curricular units. She has structured the content of the lessons so that opportunities for learning about gender issues are not lost.

SUMMARY

Curriculum

There is substantial evidence that gender differentiation exists throughout the delivery of the curriculum. During the elementary years, schools tend to structure the curriculum in a fashion that appears to be gender neutral; that is, all content is taught to all learners. However, research that measures aspects of students' participation in schooling demonstrates that a significant gap in some subject areas of curriculum exists between the genders.

By the end of elementary school, boys and girls perceive certain content areas as either "masculine" or "feminine." This identification of curriculum areas as the turf of one gender or another leads to expectations students hold for themselves. Some students, given the choice, will avoid certain content areas because they perceive it to embody characteristics that are in conflict with the role expectations for their gender. Others participate in these content areas but feel they are in alien territory.

In addition to the problems surrounding how comfortable and empowered students feel themselves to be while working within a gender-specific content area, evidence exists that strongly supports the notion that curriculum at the elementary level is not gender neutral. Historically as well as currently, test scores measuring achievement at the end of elementary school demonstrate a gender difference within certain content areas. Although not undisputed, the bulk of the research regarding reading suggests that girls, boys, and teachers consider reading to be "feminine." Some global measures of reading achievement indicate that girls as a group do better than boys in reading in elementary school.

The research findings regarding math and science are more clear-cut. Nearly without exception, studies and survey statistics indicate that during the elementary years girls and boys as groups do not demonstrate gender differences in perceptions of math and science. However, by the beginning of middle school and throughout later schooling, females come to think of math as "masculine." It is also at this time that students by gender group begin to articulate interests in different areas of science.

By the time students reach the upper grades of high school, some sorting by gender has occurred within the broader curriculum. Separation with regard to participation and attitude in both math and science is present and, especially in the area of science, achievement differences occur. When given the choice, girls are more likely than boys to opt out of higher level courses in math and science.

The result of this curricular sorting by gender group becomes apparent in college and later in career choice. Although individuals in increasing numbers are choosing occupations that may be considered non-traditional for their gender, many career areas continue to reflect considerable gender over-representation. This is especially true in career areas representing the most fundamental stereotypes: women in nurturing and child-oriented jobs and men in careers within the hard sciences such as engineering.

Instructional Materials

Students spend an enormous amount of their schooling time study-ing instructional materials. In order to help ensure gender equity in teaching, careful selection of texts and other materials is critical.

Research conducted over the past two decades has illustrated a number of gender-related problems that have existed in materi-als. Female figures have been absent from photographs and other visual displays in books. When present, females generally have been portrayed in stereotypic situations that often distort the real-ity of females' roles in society. And rather than integrate females into the primary material of the text, publishers frequently have chosen to fragment and isolate information about them, thus giv-ing the impression that the information is of lesser importance than the material in the body of the text. The research suggests that in order for students of both genders to feel they participate equally in all curricular areas instructional materials must equally and realistically represent girls and boys.

While the quality and quantity of representation in materials by gender is important, the debate about representation in the curriculum may be more critical. Whose work represents the essential knowledge that our students should study? Are the ideas of European and European-descent males, traditionally the basis for all aspects of the humanities, all that should be provided for learners? Teachers who pursue gender equity in their teaching rec-ognize that such works tend to ignore the experiences and knowl-edge of the majority of their students. Seminal works by and about women are equally critical for a more comprehensive understanding of the world.

Judy, Karen, Mary, Fred, and Pam all consider delivery of the curriculum and selection of instructional materials with regard to gender equity as important components in their teaching. Through careful selection of the content they teach and the mate-rials they choose, they work toward better gender equality in their classrooms. Male and female figures alike are included in the teaching of every unit.

CHAPTER 4

Teaching Methods

This chapter discusses aspects of some methods that play a role in facilitating gender equitable teaching. In considering this discussion, methods should be thought of within a more general context than might normally be done. In this context, method means the instructional avenue through which a teacher chooses to deliver the information. But it also is construed to include other aspects of methods a teacher chooses when constructing the learning environment in the classroom. The actions of implementing non-biased language, cooperative rather than competitive activities, programs that go beyond the limits of the classroom, and organization of the students and materials within the classroom with regard to gender equity are all methods that teachers can adopt in the pursuit of teaching in a way that is sensitive to gender equity.

Following a brief examination of recent research regarding these topics, some of the teachers' beliefs and actions are provided. Discussions with and analyses of observations of Judy, Karen, Mary, and Beth help illustrate how these teachers integrate these aspects of gender equity into their practice.

LANGUAGE

Use of language is of course an essential part of life in a classroom. The teacher conveys information to students, and students respond to the teacher and among themselves. The actual words as well as the tone used by the teacher provide direct as well as less direct messages that students integrate into their understanding of particular curricular areas and their interpretation of the world in a more general sense. One of the more obvious, although not least important, things a teacher can do with regard to teaching in a gender sensitive fashion is to select language that fully represents both genders.

All languages represent most fully the experiences of the dominant forces of a culture and tend to limit the representation of
minority groups' experiences within that culture. The English language, as well as nearly all other languages in the world today,
reflect male dominance and, generally speaking, subsume female
existence. Richardson (1989) provides a synthesis of the large
body of research that has analyzed gender dominance in the English language.

The primary theme of the research suggests that gender differentiated attitudes and beliefs about males and females are created
and reinforced due to the lack of gender balance in the structure
of the language. Six issues are striking.

Within the context of the language, females are not included
as independent figures, but rather are subordinated under that
which is male. The most obvious example of this is the use of the
generic "he" or "man." Many occupations use "man" in the title,
although in a handful of cases that has changed recently. The job
titles of "firefighter" and "letter carrier" have taken the place of
"fireman" and "mailman." Other than these examples and a few
other exceptions, the language is full of many examples that use
male pronouns and the word *man*.

When the issue of using masculine words to describe males
and females is presented to adults for consideration as an example
of gender bias, many respond that the generic usage is generally
understood by all to include both genders. They conclude, therefore, that this is a frivolous topic for serious discussion. Yet the
research is clear that, for both children and adults, this generic
interpretation tends not to hold. In fact, when presented with a
seemingly generic usage of "man" or "he," people tend to visual-
ize males rather than females, or males and females. One of the
better known activities used to illustrate this point is the "Draw
Early Cavemen" activity. When asked to do so, children do just
that. They do not include cavewomen or cavechildren in their pictures (Sadker & Sadker 1982). Other research has demonstrated
that adults respond similarly to this type of activity. When asked
to choose male or female silhouettes to correspond to sentences
that used both "man" and "he" in a generic sense, college students choose male silhouettes to illustrate the statements (DeSte-
fano 1976). These two studies represent a body of research that
concludes almost without exception that the use of "man" and
"he" in a general or generic way does not convey a mental image

to the listener of male or female. For both children and adults it sends the message that males only are meant as the subjects.

A second issue proposed by Richardson (1989) expands upon the impact of the sole usage of male-oriented language. The predominant use of male words, with occasional use of female words in specific instances, creates images, too. These are often associated with gender roles in general and occupational roles specifically. The result is perpetuation of gender stereotyping. While nearly all occupations are referred to with the generic "he," the few traditionally feminine occupations—nurse, teacher, secretary, and primary parent—nearly always are ascribed the pronoun "she." Children, who interpret language in concrete terms, immediately understand, for example, that "nurse" is feminine and "architect" is masculine, which is to say that nurses should be women and architects should be men. This is just one of any number of examples of how gender stereotyping is developed and perpetuated in young learners (MacKay 1983). While many argue that the usage of "he and she" is too cumbersome and that depersonalizing language is too awkward, the stereotyping effect of the generic usage of "he" and "man" is too well documented and powerful to consider frivolous or to ignore.

A third aspect is the trivialization in the language of that which is female. Words that are used to describe masculine people or things hold a greater weight and command greater respect than words used to describe feminine people or things. This unequal weight is well illustrated by considering when "boy" is used as compared with when "girl" is used. Rarely is "boy" used to refer to males who are no longer children. Indeed, it has taken on a distinctly negative association when considered within the context of racial epithets, such as referring to an African-American man as "boy." In contrast, female workers are often referred to as "the girls in the office" whether they are twenty or sixty-five years old. There also are many examples of words or phrases used to describe females in less than flattering terms, where no parallel terms for males exist. For instance, "girl talk" implies conversations among women that are gossipy, silly, or self-indulgent. Numerous other examples of words that imply incompetence or immaturity on the part of females are part of the English language (Richardson 1989).

The English language tends to describe females much more often than males as sexual objects, in a sexual connotation, and as the object of males' sexuality (Kramarae 1975). It is also interesting to note that in speaking of women as sexual objects, the words used are often those associated with animals: "dog, fox, ass, and chick" (Richardson 1989, 7). When men are described sexually it is as a dominant force, such as "dude, stud, and hunk" (Richardson 1989, 7).

The issue of women being portrayed as sexual objects is well illustrated through the existence of far many more words in the language that describe females sexually than those that describe males sexually. For instance, 220 terms exist that describe sexually promiscuous women, while only twenty-two exist for that description of men (Stanley 1977). There are also a number of words that at first glance appear to be gender neutral but when associated with male or female take on very different connotations. When one says "He's easy," the listener needs to be provided with a context in order to understand the meaning. On the other hand, "She's easy" has an unmistakable meaning.

Although many words define women in relationship to men, the parallel words that describe men do not relate men to women. "Mistress" and "master" once both meant one who had power over others, such as servants. Today the word "mistress" describes a woman in relationship to a man—"a woman with whom a man habitually fornicates," while "master" refers to a man who is "skilled or proficient" or powerful (Webster's New Collegiate Dictionary 1975, 737, 707). Another example of feminine words describing women in context with men is the use of "miss" and "Mrs." These are both contractions of the older version of "mistress," which once was used to refer to women regardless of their marital status. The more modern practice is to label women based on their legally defined relationship with men. "Mister" is used for all men regardless of their marital status (Richardson 1989).

The final category explored by Richardson is what she refers to as the process of "pejoration," or when a word takes on a pejorative meaning. Many pairs of words, one masculine and the other feminine, no longer have parallel meanings, such as lord and lady, baronet and dame, and governor and governess. Over time, each of these feminine terms has come to describe women in positions that are less powerful than the men's. Word pairs that illustrate more of a turn toward the pejorative are, for example, "sir" and "mister" as compared to "madam" and "mistress."

Both masculine terms are used with respect or formality, while the feminine terms are negative and sexual in meaning.

The few examples given in the six categories provide a brief account of how gender bias is built into the English language. The task of the teacher is not so much a matter of reconstructing the language in its entirety, but rather understanding the power of words on how attitudes toward the genders come to be shaped, then selecting words carefully when teaching. However undeliberately used, gender biased language sends messages to learners that perpetuate stereotyped beliefs and ideas.

COOPERATIVE ACTIVITIES

Over the past several decades, considerable attention has been paid to the differences between classrooms in which cooperation rather than the more traditional model of competition is emphasized. Researchers and many practitioners have come to understand that specific groups have experienced socialization styles that are markedly different from those of white males. One consequence of this different experience is the need for a teaching style other than what has been used traditionally. Due to several political and social events, beginning most notably in 1954 with the *Brown v. Board of Education* decision, an alternative to a competitive learning format, that of cooperative and collaborative learning, has emerged as an important teaching method. While the bulk of this inquiry has been directed toward various cultural groups, some has focused on female learners as a group. In general, the research suggests that female students as a group tend to achieve better in classrooms where learning activities are structured as cooperative ventures rather than within a competitive structure (for example, Block 1984; Fox 1976). In fact, the current research on cooperative learning techniques strongly indicates that all students, regardless of gender, culture, or socioeconomic group, benefit from this choice of teaching method (Slavin et al. 1985; Slavin 1983).

The concept of cooperation versus competition as a model for classroom learning has its roots in the work of John Dewey (1916). Dewey proposed that teachers construct classroom environments that represented the larger society. He particularly emphasized the inclusion of the concepts of democratic processes in the dynamics of the classroom interactions. In order to carry out this charge, teachers were encouraged to organize the students into small problem-solving groups in which students would work collaboratively. Cooperative behaviors and group processes were outcomes that Dewey considered essential in classrooms so that these concepts would become entrenched components in society in general.

Another early contributor to cooperative processes in classrooms was Gordon Allport (1954). Following the *Brown v. Board of Education* decision in 1954, some scholars turned their attention to the problem of intergroup acceptance. At issue was how to help students who found themselves in desegregated schools learn together and accept one another. In his seminal work, Allport suggested that several conditions needed to be present in group situations for positive interaction to occur among different groups of people. Briefly, these conditions incorporated the ideas that all representatives from each group must be accorded equal social status in the setting and that this must be directly and officially sanctioned by the authority figure. While Allport's work was directed toward integrating cultural groups, the same concepts are important to instill for cooperative work that mixes learners from any dissimilar groups, including gender. Because the social and academic structure of the school makes it clear to both genders that males are dominant, teachers incorporating gender equity in their teaching must construct classrooms where this tradition is not perpetuated.

The benefits of establishing some scheme of cooperative learning in the classroom have been documented recently by the prominent research of Slavin (for example, Slavin et al. 1985) and Johnson & Johnson (for example, Johnson & Johnson 1975). Chiefly, these benefits are as follows:

1. As interdependent relationships are created within a cooperative setting, students are motivated to work together to complete a common task

2. More positive communication modes are established among group members

3. More positive interpersonal relationships are established among group members

4. Academic achievement becomes valued by learners

5. Academic achievement can improve, particularly for high and low achievers (Arends 1988)

Teachers who choose to adopt classroom methods that reflect cooperation rather than competition establish learning environments that change the traditional dynamics of classrooms. When cooperation is emphasized, students must create the means to communicate and collaborate in order to complete the learning task. Further, students are likely to come to know one another as individuals rather than as members of a gender group. Conclusions about a person's ability no longer are dependent upon a rigid understanding of gender roles, but rather on the individual's strengths and weaknesses. When accorded equal social status, students of both genders are freed to interact and learn together in a less inhibited fashion.

Careful choice and use of non-biased language and emphasis on cooperation rather than competition in classrooms are two methods teachers can adopt that substantially contribute to gender equity, whether the teacher constructs his or her interpretation of gender equity according to an equal framework or an equitable framework. Both language and group process in cooperative settings are manipulatives that the teacher controls.

Within a context of equality, the teacher chooses language that is non-sexist. Both genders are reflected equally. Through the construction of a cooperative setting in the classroom, application of this framework ensures that all students are given all opportunities within their groups, with equal status being an important foundation for the group work.

Gender equity through an equitable framework also is reliant in part on the deliberate choice of language by the teacher as well as a carefully engineered group process within the cooperative structure. Inherent in this approach is the determination of the unempowered group as those who will be compensated for their oppressed situation. In order to combat male dominated language, anti-sexist language is adopted. This form of language usage ensures that females are over-represented. For example, females are used more often as role models than males, or the pronoun "she" would be used in a generic sense more often than "he."

The construction of cooperative groups might intentionally be manipulated such that female learners are empowered in leadership and participation positions more often than males. This would be done intentionally to counteract the tendency of male students to dominant classroom interactions and other dynamics.

Whether taken from an equal or equitable framework, language choice and creation of cooperation within the classroom are critical elements that further gender equity and are easily within the power of the teacher to implement.

A third aspect of methods that also is controlled by the teacher and has an impact on gender issues in the classroom is the physical organization of students.

ORGANIZATION

Teachers spend a great deal of their time organizing students. In the most concrete sense of the term, teachers direct students where to sit, how to line up, who to work with, and when to work at which activity. Teachers who actively reflect upon gender equity in their teaching are aware that where and with whom students do their learning creates or hampers conditions for gender equity.

The research regarding student learning and proximity to the teacher is fairly conclusive. Students who are closest to the teacher during instruction, or within what is called the "action zone," tend to participate much more in the learning activity than students seated outside of this area. Classrooms in which teachers tend to organize students in traditional ways, such as in desks in rows, illustrate action zones that incorporate the front and center, up and down the center aisle, and along the edges of the room. Students seated in these areas are the ones teachers tend to teach to, while the other students are less likely to be actively engaged in the learning (Arends 1988). Teachers who organize students in groups of tables also create similar action zones. The critical issue is how mobile the teacher is and how stationary the students are. Regardless of where students are seated, if the teacher interacts equally from all points in the classroom the negative impact of the action zone can be eliminated. Similarly, if students use their seats for activities that do not require interaction with the teacher and are mobile throughout the classroom for their learning interactions, the action zone is dismantled (Arends 1988).

There are important implications for gender equity within the context of seating of students. Adams and Biddle (1970) found students outside the action zone clearly were not participating, instead tending to be passive. They suggested that students who are more comfortable as quiet observers rather than active participants may seat themselves, when given the opportunity, outside of the action zone. While students probably do not articulate the term *action zone* or think through the issues attendant to it, they certainly can and do easily determine where the teacher is likely to look for answers and activity. They quickly learn where to sit to avoid this, if they are so inclined. In a setting where the content is associated with one gender, or where the teacher has established a pattern of interacting with one gender more often than the other, students may consciously or unconsciously seat themselves such that they participate more or less.

With regard to the formation of groups, research findings indicate that this often results in segregation. While few teachers today would construct spelling or math teams of African-American versus white, teams, work groups, and recreational groups often are formed by gender, creating a boys-against-girls situation (Grayson & Martin 1985).

Specific ways in which teachers tend to segregate students by gender include the formation of academic-oriented groups and the assignment of classroom chores. Lockheed (1981) found that in elementary classrooms only about 11 percent of the instructional time was devoted to mixed gender groups. Often academic groups represented one gender or the other. In first-grade reading groups that were mixed by gender, Wilkinson-Cherry & Subkoviak (1981) found that students of each gender tended to sit with one another and not interact with students of the other gender. Bossert (1981) studied classrooms to determine which students by gender were assigned chores. The results of the study suggested that teachers asked boys to perform manual tasks, such as moving objects, while they asked girls to take care of housekeeping chores or secretarial tasks.

A number of problems result from gender segregation within groups and from assignment of tasks based on stereotyped notions of gender roles. Students in gender segregated or biased groups tend to develop value systems that are gender differentiated and which in turn help perpetuate gender bias. Boys are more likely to value being strong and performing well academically, while girls tend to value sweetness and popularity and undervalue academic achievement, particularly as they move through early adolescence and adolescence (Clement & Eisenhart 1979; Fox 1977). Further, behaviors and attitudes that students will carry with them into the adult world are developed. Barriers are established that prevent male and female students from learning about one another and from playing together and learning the skills the others have. Finally, rather than working to open opportunities for both genders these forms of gender segregation and stereotyping help reinforce these problems in the larger society.

Teachers who demonstrate a sensitivity toward gender issues in their teaching carefully and intentionally choose methods that will further their pursuit of gender equity. The choice of words used to communicate with students, particularly in combination with teaching strategies such as collaborative group work, and the means of organizing students in the classroom for academic and other activities are important considerations.

Glimpses into the classrooms of Judy, Karen, Mary, Sean, and Beth will illustrate how these teachers incorporate gender-sensitive methods and organization into their everyday teaching.

THE TEACHERS' METHODS: LANGUAGE AND ORGANIZATION

Judy's Preschool Class

Language   Judy's interpretation of gender equity as an issue of equality is reflected in her choice of language used during the school day. As Judy teaches, she chooses non-sexist language, emphasizing the even quality of her interactions with girls and boys, which was alluded to in the discussion of interactions. For example, without exception, in the many conversations she has with her students she represents both genders when speaking generically (she or he) or makes her statement gender neutral.

Because one of the primary goals of the preschool is to help the children develop their language and ability to communicate, Judy as well as the other adults in the classroom carry on a never-ending stream of conversations with the students. During these conversations, Judy has many opportunities to influence how the students understand the world. However, consistent with her belief in the power of cognitive conflict as the most effective catalyst for change in her students' attitudes about gender roles and stereotypes, her choice of language is such that students are pressed to think about what they have done or said, rather than be "taught" Judy's personal set of values. Judy's careful choice of language is illustrated by an incident that occurred one morning.

> Several flat, cardboard dolls covered with a neutral color of felt lay on the table. Felt clothes, a dress and a shirt and pair of pants, were next to the dolls. Jennifer picked up one of the dolls and began to press the dress on it. Brian, who had been watching her, came over immediately and firmly stated,
> "That's not a girl. You can't put those clothes on this."
> Judy asked Brian to explain why he thought the doll was not a girl. In doing so, she used his words restated in the form of a question. There was no censure in her tone. "Brian, why do you think this isn't a girl? Why can't Jennifer put those clothes on this?" Brian held up the doll and pointed to the teeth that were painted on the form. "This is a man. Men have sharp teeth."
> Judy held the doll near her mouth. As she showed him her own teeth next to the doll's, Brian became agitated. Judy had sharp teeth, too. Judy waited while Brian considered what to say next. When it became apparent that he had nothing to add, she put the doll down and moved to another child.

Rather than tell Brian that sharp teeth are not an accurate indicator of either gender or of which clothes a doll can wear, Judy chose to teach the difference through creating a conflict for Brian. While Judy could not be certain that Brian had constructed a new or broader interpretation of gender, she was satisfied that he would remember the incident and it would add to his developing understanding of what males and females can do. Her choice of language and tone were intentional. They were absolutely gender neutral, both with regard to the actual words used as well as the lack of value judgment placed on Brian because he believed pants and sharp teeth belonged only on males.

Organization   Consistent with the preschool goal of enabling students in their endeavors during the school day, Judy allows her students to organize themselves, regardless of the activity. The classroom is furnished with various centers within which the children work. They move and work independently, rather than at Judy's direction. After recommending a course of action for the student to take, Judy steps back and allows the student to choose.

She adamantly refuses to engineer students into social or academic learning situations, even when doing so would likely change a child's behavior, at least in the short run.

The eight girls and six boys in Judy's class work in pairs or alone. In every case of two children doing an activity together, the children are of the same gender. Of the two times during the morning when the students come together as a group (snack and story time), they always seat themselves in two groups—one of girls and the other of boys.

The students segregate themselves according to gender during their time in the centers as well. On only one occasion were girls found building with the blocks:

> Four girls, holding hands and walking so closely together they seemed to be interconnected, approached the corner of the room that housed the blocks. Two boys were standing on the periphery of the area. The girls noticed the boys and bent their heads to whisper. Some kind of agreement was reached, and they turned to the large cardboard blocks, which resembled bricks. With little discussion, they began to build a wall of bricks, which separated them from the boys who had moved in a bit to gain some access to the materials. When the wall was completed, they began their second project, which was to construct a house.

The first item of business for the girls literally had been to separate themselves from the boys. That done, they could do what they wanted with the blocks.

With the exception of this incident, boys dominated the block center. Over a period of more than ten hours of observation, girls were found in the block area only for about fifteen minutes. All of the boys used the blocks at least some of the time during the mornings, as opposed to only four girls using them once. Clearly, both boys and girls had determined that the blocks were masculine territory.

Another incident that illustrates the students' perceptions of gender-specific tasks took place one morning. A mother of one of the children spent time in the class working with students preparing the snack (peanut butter balls) for that day. Although each child was offered an opportunity to work with her, the only ones who did so were five girls. No child received extra persuasion to become involved. If they indicated no interest, they found something else to do. The cooking activity became strictly a girls' activity. As the children exercised their freedom of choice of activity, the result was gender segregation both in who they interacted and played with and in how they classified activities according to gender.

When asked to comment about this, Judy described both developmental issues with the children as well as her philosophy. Developmentally, many of the children, especially the younger and less mature of the group, are still learning how to socialize with other children. As a result, they often play alone or with one other child. When asked if she felt it would be appropriate for her to direct children to interact with other specific children (for example, a boy with a girl), Judy reiterated her thoughts about providing total choice for the students so long as they were not engaging in destructive behavior.

While Judy sees herself as an important model for and teacher of gender equity, she does not believe in indoctrinating the students according to a "proper" set of values. Instead, through her use of absolutely gender neutral language and her provision for self direction by the children, she provides a learning environment in which traditional gender role expectations and stereotypes are not reinforced. In a sense, she provides a clean slate for the children to fill in as they are encouraged to verbalize their actions and their thoughts. When these actions and thoughts reflect gender bias, Judy takes the opportunity to question the children about their assumptions and to examine facts, such as in the sharp-tooth incident. What she will not do is direct the students into interactions that might satisfy her agenda regarding gender equity.

Karen's Kindergarten Class

In contrast to Judy, Karen is not at all hesitant to intervene, direct, and engineer in order to address gender equity in her classroom. She too makes careful use of language, but does so in a way different from Judy. She also considers issues of student and classroom organization as vital components in teaching in gender sensitive ways. Unlike Judy, she constructs activity and interactive situations for the students, removing much of their freedom of choice but in doing so insures that gender segregation cannot exist in the classroom.

Language   As illustrated in the discussion of teacher-initiated interactions and the discussion about materials, Karen addresses issues related to gender equity directly with her students. One of her more interesting techniques, which combines deliberate choice of method and language, is demonstrated during story reading time. Karen often uses folk tales as the material for story reading. Her method is to read the book as it was written, with the gender of the main character unaltered. She then reads the story with the character as the other gender. This is an example of actual "teaching" of a gender issue. The following story-reading session was typical.

> The Chinese New Year was approaching. All activities were centered around the study of Chinese culture. The story for the day, a Chinese folk tale, was about a boy who left for an adventure, which included duck hunting. Karen read the story through as it was printed. Following the reading she paused. "Who was the main character in the story?" she asked. The children chorused with the boy's name. "Could a girl have been the main character and done the same things that the boy did?" The group answered "Yes." "Let's see how it sounds with a girl as the main character." "Let's call her Ling." Karen reread the story with Ling as the main character.

During other story-reading sessions, the selection presented a female main character. After the initial reading of the story, Karen asked the same questions and followed the procedure of re-reading the story with a male as the main character.

Although in the retelling of these events the scene depicted may seem tedious and redundant, the students enjoyed the stories being told twice. Further, Karen's intentional choice of method and language usage created visual images for the children each time, which reinforced the concept that both a male and a female could do whatever was related in the story. Actually placing each gender in the lead of the story, rather than just telling the children that it was possible for the other gender to replace the lead character, created a more powerful image for the listeners than if Karen had simply told the students it could be so.

In the ongoing conversations and other interactions Karen has with her students, she is careful to use non-biased language. "He or she" is used in the place of a generic "he." She also has made a point to erase from her vocabulary "guys" as a generic term. As she pointed out, the students objected, saying that word only refers to boys. Instead she has adopted "people" as the word she uses when seeking the attention of the entire group.

Karen uses non-biased language in the ordinary routine in her classroom. She also uses specific language to directly confront gender bias within the context of various lessons. She strongly believes that inherent in her role as teacher, particularly in the culturally heterogeneous school in which she works, is the job of drawing her students' attention to bias and intolerance. In addressing these issues directly, she helps her students learn what it is and how not to be a party to it themselves.

Karen's methods of organizing her students complements and reinforces her use of language and the goals she seeks to meet. A strong sense of community exists in the classroom, where cooperation and collaboration prevail.

Organization   At the beginning of the school year, Karen organizes the students into committees. These committees are designated by color and are the result of intentional mixing of cultures, socioeconomic backgrounds, academic readiness, and genders. Committees travel through the centers as a group. But the committee structure is more than an expedient means of moving children around the room. Students within the committee are responsible for helping one another both socially and academically. For example, the Blue Committee was not finished at a center until everyone on that committee had helped clean up. The willingness to help one another was apparent across committees as well.

> Tanya's committee of four had been working at the cutting center. The three other children had finished and moved on to another activity. As Tanya finished her work, she looked up and noticed that scraps of paper and scissors littered the table.
> "Karen, no one else is here to help with the cleaning." Karen suggested that Tanya tell her committee to return to the table and help her. John, a member of a different committee, stood nearby. "I'll help you, Tanya." While Tanya and John cleaned, another student from a third committee came to the table and also helped.

Girls and boys work together toward the same goal, in this case cleaning the table. There were many other examples of integration of the genders. During dismissal for recess, lunch, or other activities out of the classroom, Karen chose a variety of categories to group the students in the line by the door; for example.

> "Let's see. Today, those who have jackets that zipper may line up first. Next, those with buttons may line up. Remember, form pairs."

As the children moved to the door, without exception the pairs that formed were mixed. Girls and boys, Hispanic and white, and neighborhood and non-neighborhood children stood together at the door holding hands.

Through her years of teaching kindergarten, Karen has developed some creative ways of assigning classroom jobs. For example, at the beginning of each school year she places each child's picture on a small card, which is color coded according to committee assignment. During the class meeting, which is held on the rug at the start of each morning, Karen shuffles the cards, and several children take turns picking one at random for a job for that day. In that way, regardless of the traditional gender association with a job, both boys and girls may be assigned to it. Plant and animal care, collection of materials, and all other jobs are rotated.

Tasks that come up during the activities of the day are assigned in a general fashion.

> A boy and a girl were completing their coloring assignments at a center. Most of the students in the room were finished with their activities and were getting ready to go to lunch. Karen looked around the room and noticed that several housekeeping tasks needed to be taken care of. "Kathy and Davis, will one of you please stack the chairs and one of you straighten the books?" Kathy began to stack the four chairs in the corner as Davis carefully placed books neatly on the shelf.

The children took on the task they preferred. There was no indication, on the part of the teacher or the children, that Davis should have been moving the heavy chairs while Kathy should take care of the neatness problem.

Karen has integrated gender equity into her teaching through a framework of equality. Her methods of doing so, both through language usage and organizational structure, vary considerably from Judy's. The principal difference is her belief in directly addressing gender issues with the children. She does this literally through the adoption of language that points out to children aspects of traditional gender role expectations, such as in the example of the dual reading of the folk tales. She also does this through intentional mixing of students in academic and social groups. She constructs situations that will require children of both genders (as well as other group identities) to work and learn together. These activities require cooperation and collegial support.

The results of these methods are easily observed. Unself-consciously, children work together and help each other in an integrated group. They also are aware, on a very conscious level, of what constitutes sexist language, to the extent that an unsuspecting outsider casually using a generic "he" is told in no uncertain terms that the use of that word in that way is inappropriate. Karen directly teaches her students about gender equity, with an emphasis on the notion that gender is never a limiting factor.

Mary's Third-Grade Class

Mary also uses language and organization in specific and intentional ways in order to address gender equity. Consistent within the framework of equality, Mary's choice of language offers both boys and girls the same representation in all aspects of classroom activity. However, while she is very conscious of the impact of organization of students on issues of gender equity, she is less willing than Karen to intervene in some matters of choice by her students.

Language   As with Judy and Karen, Mary is careful to use non-sexist or gender-neutral language in her conversations with students. When addressing the group at large, she has chosen the word *people* to include all of the students. In statements that require a pronoun used generically, she habitually uses "he or she." These are language choices she has made for some time and says them routinely. However, her use of language in some learning situations demonstrates her reflection on the impact her words will have on the students regarding their thinking about gender.

> Approximately one half of the class left the room for P.E. Ten students from different classes entered for math instruction with the remainder of Mary's class. These students had been identified as students requiring additional enrichment in math—all high achievers. The students, eleven boys and nine girls, clustered around Mary's front table by the chalkboard. Several word problems were written on the board. The wording of the problems was similar. One read: "Kate, Brandon, Peter, and Jane were on the trail to Santa Fe. Brandon's team followed Kate's. Kate refused to be last, Jane was second in line, just ahead of Kate. List the people in order of their wagons."

In all lessons, such as this one, that which require specific language, Mary chooses situations, using the names of the students in the class, in which males and females all do the same things. She deliberately chooses scenarios that constitute traditionally masculine and traditionally feminine settings; from the general and other officers in charge of a military school to the homemaker in charge of preparing weekly budgets. Both girls and boys find themselves depicted in traditional and non-traditional settings.

While Mary deliberately uses language to shape learning contexts into ones that are non-sexist and occasionally anti-sexist, she intervenes far less when it comes to engineering her students into physical spaces where they are compelled to work with students of the other gender.

Organization   When asked about how she determines seating and grouping of students, Mary speaks of developmental and philosophical issues in much the same way as Judy. Mary feels that, at this age, students are happiest working with a partner of the same gender. To intervene in this would create unnecessary conflict. Philosophically, she believes that both genders of students receive the same learning opportunities and experiences regardless of where they sit and with whom they interact.

> Their regularly assigned desks are most often assigned by me. Girls sit next to a girl, and boys most often sit next to a boy. At this age they really do like the same sex partner. And we do partner things. But at the table, they do things with girls and boys. Sometimes they'll number off, random grouping; sometimes I assign groups. A lot of times I say choose your own partner or groups of three and those are most apt, but not always to be same sex. I don't really see any real advantage in always making sure they're mixed. Especially when the kids want to separate, as long as they can come together later. Like in our wagon groups, they had to put down names, knowing they would have to travel in wagons that would have both men and women. They had to put down names of people they thought would be dependable, and their choices were not by gender.

Because she is sensitive about equalizing learning opportunities for both genders, Mary has adopted two means of organizing her students which create different dynamics among students and between students and herself during different times of the day, and which encourage collaboration among the students.

Mary creates a variety of action zones throughout the day. Although students are assigned seats at their tables (two tables of four each are pushed together lengthwise), they spend only a part of their time there. With the introduction of each new activity, students move to a different part of the room. For example, one math session required the students to cluster around a table in the front of the room, then move to the rug area, then scatter about the room in pairs to play a math game. During the first and second segments of the math lesson, Mary was stationary. Different students were seated close to her for each activity. While the students played the math game, Mary moved from group to group systematically, monitoring each group for the same amount of time. The learning resource, in this case Mary herself, was more evenly distributed among both genders than if all the teaching had taken place in the same location. These organizational schemes allow Mary to interact with all of the students on a fairly even basis, and also allow a great deal of freedom of choice for the students; they can choose where they will place themselves and with whom they will work.

Mary works to create an atmosphere of cooperation and collaboration in the classroom within a school district that emphasizes individual student achievement. While it is not accurate to characterize the school as one where competition is the only factor present, it is accurate to say that achievement test scores, ability grouping, and other indicators of competition are heavily concentrated upon. Students in Mary's class spend approximately a third of their time working independently. The individual work is generally done when assessment or diagnostic information is required. During the instructional part of the various lessons, Mary constructs her lessons such that students work together. While she does not use cooperative learning in the formal sense of the term, pairs and small groups of students spend much of their day working in interdependent learning situations. When the groups are formulated according to tables, as they are more often than not, the boys and girls in the group depend on each other for completion of a task. They grow to know each other individually and are less likely to think in gender-stereotypical ways about the abilities or behaviors of girls or boys.

A second collaborative means of classroom organization Mary uses is drawing the students into active participation in all learning activities during the day. In addition to continuously questioning and soliciting their opinion, Mary organizes the students into a body whose input is considered and used. While the students do not govern the classroom, they are asked to recommend how to go about learning certain things or to set up specific situations so they feel more in charge of their learning. Their opinions and recommendations are sought and implemented.

> The artists in residence for the third grade were a popular singing group. The task was for the group and Mary's class was to write a musical presentation that would tell the story of a Mexican folk tale, *La Yrona*. The singing group helped the students with the production of their presentation, but it was up to Mary and the class to write the words.

Mary provided only minimal direction while the students wrote all the songs and determined appropriate places on the stage for each actor. The musical production was entirely of the students' making. While this example is not one of a routine classroom activity, it illustrates how student participation and input on a collaborative basis were used. Similar scenarios were commonplace during the more routine lessons, where decisions about where or how to address certain aspects of lessons were made by the students.

During times of student input, especially when it will affect the entire group, Mary is careful to consider whose ideas are incorporated. In this case, she chooses to engineer the situation. So that students who might have a tendency to dominate the discussion do not do so, she intentionally selects students so everyone will have an opportunity to make her or his voice heard. On a rotating basis that appears uncontrived, she provides each student with a chance to be an active participant. The end result is a collaborative climate, in which each student is an active member in the learning community.

Mary's commitment to gender equity through a framework of equality is demonstrated through her use of non-biased language, as illustrated when she incorporates girls and boys equally in the language of the lesson. Her organizational techniques provide an environment of cooperation and collaboration, as well as active student participation in nearly all aspects of the learning. She carefully monitors her control of student participation to ensure that neither individuals nor gender groups dominate. She deliberately alternates among the students on an even or equal basis so that each student will be incorporated into the dynamics of the learning. In this way she believes she provides equal access to all learning resources and opportunities and that she is enhances gender equity in her teaching.

Sean's Middle-School Art Class

As noted in chapter 1, Sean's principal means of addressing gender equity is through his scheme of classroom management. However, inherent in the management techniques are attention to choice of language and well-orchestrated organization of the students. He believes that both issues require careful consideration in order to ensure that each student receives equal treatment and has a chance to participate in the same way in the learning processes.

Language Sean's use of language is deliberately neutral. During his ongoing monitoring of students in the production portion of the class, his words of critique and encouragement address the project at hand and are nearly identical from one student to the next. His use of pronouns also are non-sexist, reflecting both genders when the sense of the statement is generic.

Sean believes that to some extent he nudges his female students into considering issues of gender equity. He often teases his students as a means of maintaining a casual atmosphere in the room. Sometimes he attempts to combine the two.

> Sometimes I say things tongue-in-cheek about gender equity. But I have to double-check. For instance, I will make a statement like, "That's not bad for a girl" and see if I get a rise out of the girl. Nowadays I do. The girls say "What do you mean?" and I say, "Oh, you're awake. That's good to know." But I'm cautious about doing that, because I'm not sure how it will be taken.

Through this teasing mechanism, Sean of course is implying to his female students that the stereotype of females not being as competent as males is not in operation in his classroom. But he may have reason to be cautious in using this form of consciousness raising. On one occasion, he praised a female student, and she and her female partner appeared to be offended.

> Sean examined the papier maché mask that Susan held up for his inspection. "Good girl," he said. As he moved on to the next table, the girl turned to her partner and muttered, "He made it sound like he was talking to a dog."

Perhaps Sean uses "Good girl" and "Good boy" evenly as a means of addressing students who are progressing nicely, and in that way applies the label equally. In fact, several times he praised boys with "Good boy." Nonetheless, it sounded awkward to these female students and they took it to be less than complimentary.

Organization   While it may be argued that some of Sean's techniques in using language to further gender equity in the classroom do not further his goal of teaching within an equal framework, his means of organizing students so that they all receive equal resources during the class are powerful. When asked about how he seats his students, Sean responded this way:

> Usually when they come in the first day of the quarter the desks will be in semicircles. They won't be in traditional rows. The kids will come in, and I'll say, "You may sit where you wish." I don't usually put them into groups of four. I give them the opportunity not to talk too much. They get seated, then make folders. I don't have a seating chart. They put their names on the folders. I tell them when the folders are on the counter, they come in and get the folder and sit any where they want to. If the folders are on the desks, that means that's where I expect them to sit. That may be for just one day, or it may be for longer. I also use it as a disciplinary measure. I move the folder, not the kid. When I'm in a rush, I may assign them arbitrarily, so it comes out very mixed then.

Seating the students according to their folders has the benefit of helping Sean keep track of which students are not progressing in the assignments as well as the others. He reviews the folders before each group of students enters class in order to monitor their progress. He can then place a student who may need a calming influence next to one who is moving on to the next phase of the project. This means of organization also has the effect of mixing the students by gender as well as other classifications. On each observation occasion, the students in the classes were seated in very different places and next to people they had not been near previously.

While students are responsible for completing their own assignments in the class, they also are expected to help one another. Cooperation is a rule in the classroom that Sean periodically reiterates. During the construction of the papier maché masks, it was common to see one student who had finished a portion turn to his or her partner and offer to help. The partners often represented pairs who were not alike in gender, culture, special needs, and socioeconomic backgrounds. Students worked in this fashion as a matter of course. There also was no pattern of particular students providing help to the same slower students on a regular basis. Each observation revealed different students who were the helpers and those being helped.

Finally, as each class session drew to an end, Sean monitored cleanup. Pairs or groups of four students who were done cleaning their area went to other tables to help those students clean. On one occasion, Sean walked around in the classroom to remind students to put materials away.

> "Everybody clean-up. Remember, you're helping each other. I see some people who think they're done because they've cleaned their own things. Everybody needs to help everyone."

Sean reflects upon both his choice of language and his means of organizing students as components of integrating gender equity into his teaching. He believes his language is for the most part neutral, although on occasion he tries to provoke students into thinking about gender issues through the use of blatantly sexist language. In the several examples cited, it is not clear that his usage of language in this manner achieves his goal. However, because he is someone who is conscious of the power of his words, especially with regard to gender equity, he is likely to consider student and peer feedback as he continuously refreshes his teaching strategies.

Sean's means of organization are effective in moving toward his goal of treating all his students equally. He engineers the students' seating so that each student interacts with each of the other people in the classroom at some point.

The spirit of cooperation and collaboration help all the students feel enabled. Each of Sean's students has the opportunity to succeed, and nearly all do. This includes the special-needs students, who experience failure in many of their other classes. The result of Sean's organizational methods that enhance gender equity in his teaching is a highly integrated learning environment across gender. Each student works with a variety of classmates throughout the duration of the nine-week course. Mixing and matching students based on their progress with the project at hand allows boys and girls to work together in the class, without creating a contrived scheme.

Consistent with Sean's interpretation of gender equity as an issue of equality, he has constructed a classroom in which his students benefit from the teaching resources in an equal fashion. He summarized his sense of working with students within an equality framework this way:

> Maybe it's just the equality of kids. It has something to do with appreciating each one as a student, as a very important human being.

Beth's Middle-School Science Class

Although Beth's overall interpretation of gender equity, through an equitable framework as opposed to one of equality, is at variance with the other teachers profiled, she does share some of the same orientation in considering her choice of language as well as in her scheme of classroom organization.

Language   Beth also carefully considers her choice of language as a means to further her integration of gender equity into her teaching. The way she speaks to the students, the tone and the actual words used, help create a climate that she perceives to be productive. She sets out and succeeds in establishing an atmosphere of caring, friendliness, and control. Her caring is illustrated by her interest in her students' life outside as well as inside the classroom. For example, a student whose substance-abusing father locked her out of the house spoke to Beth about her difficulties in completing her homework. Beth and the student took time to solve the immediate problem of homework. Later on, Beth addressed the larger problem in the home with the girl and another school professional. The fact that this conversation as well as similar ones with other students took place suggests that students place a high degree of trust in Beth. A strong sense of comfort and belonging permeates the classroom. Beth answers the students' concerns and problems with language that reinforces their status as people, not just as students positioned in the room ready to learn science.

Another language technique Beth employs is her choice of words that are casual rather than formal. This is done for several reasons. Many students enter the class somewhat mystified or even fearful about science. The informality of her approach helps put the students at ease. Beth tends to use early-adolescent language initially in explaining the lesson. After the concepts are learned, she substitutes scientific terms.

A second motive in establishing a relaxed environment is to shorten the status gulf between herself as teacher and the young people as students. She believes that in order for the students to be their most productive they must not feel intimidated by an unnecessary power relationship, which some teachers impose over their students.

While the description of a relaxed and caring climate in Beth's classroom might produce a vision of a group of students out of control, the situation is quite the opposite. Students learn from the beginning that they are cared for as people in general, but most especially as learners. Beth's high expectations and demands, particularly for the girls, result in a very high degree of student engagement during the classes. Her use of assertive discipline is swift and consistent among the students. While the atmosphere is relaxed and casual, the students know the behavioral guidelines and the consequences of violating them.

Beth uses non-sexist language and helps her students do the same. On several occasions, different students used "he" or "man" in a generic sense.

> The first part of the lesson about global warming took the form of questions and answers about the students' prior information. "What was the global temperature like during the Ice Age?" Beth asked the class. Maria was called on. "It was cold due to the glaciers. The cave men had to have a life style that was adaptable to the cold." Beth agreed with the idea, if not the actual language. "Right, Maria. Cavepeople had to develop many things in their lives that could accommodate the cold."

With the correction of "cave man" to "cave people," Beth subtly reminded Maria of the more inclusive term. As Beth moved on to another question, Maria nodded and then mouthed the words "cave people" as if to reinforce it.

Another example of non-sexist language used by Beth that is similar to that of many of the other teachers is the choice of the word *folks* when addressing the group at large. While the concentration on non-sexist words appears fairly inconsequential to many people, Beth believes that the use of these words is important as one of the components of gender equity in her classroom.

Organization   Examination of Beth's classroom organization reveals that she shares some of the orientation of teachers such as Judy and Mary. In general, she believes that students should have choice in some matters as long as their learning is unimpeded. Another organizational tactic she shares with others is her emphasis on collaborative work among the students.

As a rule, Beth does not engineer her seating arrangement in order to provide for a gender mix. But she does give careful consideration to who is seated where and the implications for the action zone during periods of direct group instruction.

> I don't usually intervene in how kids seat themselves. Although if it's a front-back issue, then I do. Because front-back sometimes dictates who I pay attention to. But if it's a left-right issue, then I don't. I like the kids to have fun in my class. So if they're sitting with their friends and they can do the work, that's OK.
>
> One other thing I do is separate them into groups. They sit at tables of between three and five. I can add or juggle kids around into a group if that helps the group work better. I do this especially if there's a difficult project and it's going to last a long time. Then I assign them so there's some kind of gender balance.

When given the choice, Beth's students tend to segregate themselves along gender lines. Only one table in each of the two classes had a mixed-gender group. The positioning of the groups by gender is scattered. There are "girl tables" and "boy tables" in both the front, back, and sides of the room. Beth is not particularly concerned about the issue of gender segregation at tables. She focuses on her methods of drawing the students into the discussions and her monitoring techniques as the more important devices to ensure that her students are engaged. These techniques also are the means Beth uses to emphasize female participation in all aspects of the lesson. While Beth monitors the groups in a fairly even fashion, she pulls the female students into the discussions more frequently than the male students, and presses them a bit harder than the boys for quality in their work.

A final component of Beth's organizational scheme that is similar to a number of the other teachers is a focus on collaboration and cooperation. Perhaps to a greater extent than any of the other teachers, Beth has constructed a situation where nearly all learning that takes place in the classroom is done in a cooperative setting. The only activities that are done on an individual basis are note taking and test taking.

A project is the focal point of each unit. The projects are completed through the cooperative efforts of group members. While group members do not have tasks that are assigned only to them, as is the case with formal cooperative learning (for example, Johnson & Johnson 1975), Beth's monitoring effectively assures that each person in the group is contributing. During periods of project work, Beth moves from one group to the next, carefully watching each person to check for involvement. When the projects are successfully completed, each group member receives points that contribute to their final grade. During the hours of observation when project work was going on every student, with one exception, was engaged the entire time. (The one student isolated herself in the corner and spent her time staring into space. Beth described the student as having several problems. She was a non-English speaker, and she refused to work with any of the other students who were bilingual and could help translate. Up to that point, Beth had not worked out a way to incorporate her into the group).

Through Beth's careful choice of language and classroom organization, an atmosphere of caring, high expectation, and carefully controlled limits has been established. Students work cooperatively and continuously. Beth's methods may appear quite similar to those of the teachers who interpret gender equity through a framework of equality rather than an equitable framework. The difference is apparent when her interactions with the students are analyzed. The emphasis on empowerment of girls in her science classes is demonstrated through her unequal distribution of resources. She believes the girls need more, and she provides it for them. This issue is examined in more detail in chapter 5.

Gender equity is a driving force in Beth's professional life. While she believes that the methods she employs in her classroom help shape how girls and boys perceive themselves as well as others along gender lines with regard to academic and personal abilities, she devotes a substantial amount of time to an additional means or method of addressing gender equity. Through the development of Women's Month activities and other special girls-only functions, she pursues gender issues on a scale larger than her classroom.

Several years ago, Beth learned from a friend in another city about a program in her school that set aside time before, during, and after school when forums, discussion groups, and recreational activities were held for the female students. The idea was to allow the girls to learn about themselves and their unlimited opportunities. The program also allowed for a shift of focus from the traditional celebration of male achievement on the playing field and in the classroom to female issues and achievement.

> A friend of mine teaches in Phoenix. She told me about what they are doing there. Another teacher here was very supportive, and we got things going. Some of the activities are just for fun, where there are all women. The university volleyball team came out. And we took the girls to see the women's university basketball team play.
>
> We also have lunch forums. They get announced ahead of time. One was about the different pressure points on girls and boys. Another was on domestic violence. Quite a few of the teachers go and are very supportive. Another thing we do is show a film in the seventh-grade language arts and social studies classes. It's about a son who wants to be a dancer and a daughter who wants to be a lawyer. It makes a point about parental expectation about gender.
>
> We do a mother/daughter luncheon. It's great. We had sixty girls and their mothers this year. They were in heaven. They got waited on for a change. I told a story about women achieving against great odds. A girl from school read a poem. I talked about how Women's Month got started, and that we were here to celebrate what we do have, and the struggle women have had in the past.

Given that nearly all the girls with whom Beth works live in homes that are strongly patriarchal, Hispanic and Tohono O'Odom (a native American nation in Southern Arizona), she feels it is particularly important to stress to her female students that there is a vast array of options for them in the larger culture. As in nearly all underclass neighborhoods, poverty, early pregnancy, dropping out, and a number of domestic problems are prevalent among the families of her students. Beth sees Women's Month and other special activities as a small antidote to these problems that her female students often face. Beth's goal is not to remove the girls from their culture, but instead to show them the means to succeed outside of it if they choose that path. Despite the inherent conflict between some of the cultural practices of the families and the message of the Women's Month activities, which have to do with empowering women, Beth has encountered little resistance from parents in providing these enriching activities for their daughters.

While nearly all of Beth's methods are intended to further gender equity in her teaching practice, the most distinctive method
she uses is the ongoing program of special activities and the high-
lighted functions in March during Women's Month. She believes
the girls need the opportunity to be among themselves, removed
from the dynamics produced when boys are present.

> The girls need to have a voice and to see who they are. When
> they're with the boys, they don't get a chance to make decisions.
> The boys usually dominate. That's why it's so important to give
> them this.

SUMMARY

The careful use of language, implementation of cooperative activities, and consideration of student organization are all important
methods that teachers choose and control in their pursuit of integrating gender equity into their teaching. Language that is non-
sexist or anti-sexist allows for representation of all class members,
male and female. Research in this area has demonstrated that the
traditional use of masculine terms in a generic sense does not provide for inclusion of females. Adults and children develop imagery
that is masculine. Although seemingly innocuous, the use of "he"
as an inclusive term becomes an exclusionary act.

Judy, Karen, Mary, and Beth all use language carefully chosen
for its gender neutrality or for its ability to portray females and
males in all situations. Judy and Beth are both conscious of using
language that is neutral with regard to gender. Karen and Mary
use language in a way that addresses gender equity in a more
direct fashion. References to females and males are done in such a
way as to portray both genders in all situations as well as to show
them reflected in non-traditional settings or activities.

Classrooms where the emphasis is on cooperation rather than
strictly on competition have climates that produce better learners,
both in general as well as in ways that are important for gender
equity purposes. Research strongly suggests that males and particularly females tend to achieve more academically in collaborative
classrooms. There are social dividends as well. When compelled
to work together or in other ways to be interdependent, students
are more likely to learn about their peers according to individual
characteristics rather than in gender-stereotypical ways. Karen,

Mary, Sean, and Beth have composed classrooms that depend on these interconnections. Competition is minimal and cooperation is the focus.

Finally, the actual organization of the students and their place-ment in the action zone are important issues to consider. Researchers have found that teachers who unreflectively create groups of students tend to have learning or recreation groups that are gender segregated. The result of such groups is a them-against-us or, more specifically, boys-against-girls climate. Such a climate hinders rather than facilitates learning about one another. Gender-based grouping also lends itself to perpetuation of gender-role stereotyping, both by the teacher and the students themselves.

The degree to which the teachers profiled are comfortable with overt engineering of the placement of students in the room varies. Karen and Sean have devised different ways of placing stu-dents in the learning activities that are not obvious to the stu-dents, yet allow the teachers control over who sits where and who interacts with whom. Judy clearly does not directly engineer her students into contact with other particular students. She is opposed to intervening in this matter of student choice. Mary and Beth take a somewhat middle-of-the-road position in their think-ing about the physical placement of students in the room. In some situations, they allow their students to choose where they will be and with whom they will interact. For other activities, these teachers manufacture groups that result in a gender balance.

All of the teachers discussed in this chapter are sensitive to the influence of the action zone. Because of the emphasis of interac-tion with individual students in Judy's room, the issue of the action zone is almost moot. Judy moves to each child and has conversations with her or him. In Karen's room, the greater part of the day is spent with the various groups of children moving to her. Only during times of group meetings does Karen interact with the entire group. For Karen, the action zone surrounds her as the small groups of children work with her on a rotating basis. Mary moves the site of instruction often throughout the day. The result is that those students who were most closely contained in the action zone for instruction for one activity are replaced by another group for the next activity. Sean and Beth move them-selves, principally during monitoring periods. Because their classes spend the bulk of the class period in project work, the result of their constant movement during their monitoring is to engage themselves with the individual students. Their action zones move with them.

Implemented in isolation, these three methods may appear to have modest importance in their influence on integrating gender equity into classroom teaching. Yet the research is convincing about the impact of these methods, and they require careful consideration. Use of non-sexist or anti-sexist language, emphasis on cooperative activities, and organization of students that is sensitive to equal or equitable participation by students of both genders are critical components in the larger scheme of gender equity in classrooms.

CHAPTER 5

Teacher Interactions

Most teachers do not intentionally differentiate learning opportunities for their students by gender. Much of what constitutes gender inequity in classroom practices and interactions is subconscious and subtle. In order to fully understand their effectiveness, teachers must become sensitive to the tendency to teach some students differently than others.

One of the most powerful and subtle influences teachers exert with students is through the quality and quantity of interactions. As the research below illustrates, teachers tend to interact differently with their students based on the students' gender. In general, teacher interactions allow for male dominance in classrooms. Further, this appears to be the case regardless of the age of the students, the gender of the teacher, the years of experience of the teacher, or the subject matter being taught.

A sampling of the research follows that illustrates that the quantity and quality of teacher interactions varies by student gender. The remainder of the chapter takes us into the classrooms of Judy, Karen, Mary, Sean, and Beth. Their interpretations of the issues surrounding gender-biased interactions, as well as their approaches to counter this aspect of gender bias, vary considerably.

Quantity of Interactions

1. Teachers tend to give boys more attention, both positive and negative. Boys receive more of the teacher's time than girls.

2. Male students tend to initiate more interactions than female students with their teachers, seeking and receiving more teacher attention.

Quality of Interactions

1. Male students who are perceived of as high achievers receive more academic-related teacher interactions than their female counterparts.

2. Teachers tend to provide interactions with male students that help them learn tasks, while teachers are likely to do the tasks for the female students.

3. Males are more often asked questions by teachers that require a higher degree of thinking than are female students.

QUANTITY OF INTERACTIONS

As the following research data illustrate, male students simply get *more* than do female students in most classrooms.

In general, research suggests that boys command more attention, both positive and negative, from teachers. Over time, research findings have been fairly consistent in these results. For example, a study conducted by Meyer and Thompson (1956) reported findings that indicated boys were more likely to receive both positive and negative comments from their teachers than were girls. A 1973 study by Good, Sikes, and Brophy indicated similar conclusions. Simpson and Erickson (1983) studied teachers' verbal and non-verbal praise and criticism in relationship to several personal characteristics of students that might affect the amount of attention they gave to students. One of these characteristics was gender. Sixteen female first-grade teachers were observed for their interactions with their students. The interactions were divided into six categories: verbal praise; verbal criticism or rejection of work, ideas, or behavior; verbally neutral behavior; non-verbal praise such as pleasant tone or pleasant facial expressions; non-verbal criticism such as frowns or glares; and non-verbally neutral behavior. Among the white teachers (half of the sample), there was a clear distinction by gender of student in their interaction pattern. Boys received more interactions, verbal and non-verbal, than did girls. Interestingly, the gender differentiation did not hold for the African-American teachers. They did not interact with one gender more often than the other. Although outside of the scope of the material considered here, the authors of this study suggest some difference in gender role perceptions may exist between white and African American teachers, which could in turn influence their interaction patterns. However, it would be important to consider the cultural background of each of the teachers in this study before the cultural or racial variable could be used as a predictive indicator. In other words, simply because one is African-American does not indicate that he or she holds particular beliefs. Therefore, one cannot globally state that African American teachers hold fewer gender stereotypes than do teachers of other cultures.

Irvine (1985) chose students in grades kindergarten through seven to examine teacher feedback or communication from the teacher to the students regarding their classroom progress. She looked at academic, behavioral, and procedural verbal interactions, which were coded as positive, negative, or neutral. Irvine found that males received more attention in sheer volume. She also reported that the male students received more feedback from the teachers in the areas of praise, negative behavior feedback, neutral procedural feedback, and non-academic feedback. The results of this study reaffirm that boys simply receive more in the classroom.

A study conducted in Australia examined teacher interactions based on gender as well as other variables. Thirty preschool teachers, twenty-five women and five men, were observed working with four- and five-year-olds. Ebbeck (1984) found that the teacher interacted more often with boys than girls. The results of the study also reflected a difference in interaction depending on the curriculum area. Some curricula or activity areas were heavily used by the boys, while others were more frequently used by the girls. The only part of the children's day that showed even interactions by gender was snack time. The curriculum preferences by gender were very pronounced and quite stereotypical. Art and dramatic play were the only two areas preferred by girls. Blocks, construction, story, discussion, sand, and climbing were the dominant choices of the boys. By some means, the girls came to be limited to only two curricular areas. The boys, on the other hand, dominated the bulk of the curricula list. The results of this study showed that the boys' domination extended from holding most of the teacher's attention to being a more powerful presence in the overall school day than the girls.

Irvin (1986) examined interactions initiated by the teacher as well as those initiated by students. In addition to race and grade level, gender was again a variable under consideration. The teachers and students studied were in grades kindergarten through five. With regard to the issue of differentiation of teacher interaction by gender, the results were consistent with Irvin's earlier study (1985), as well as the bulk of the research done by others on this topic. In general, male students were found to initiate more inter-actions with their teachers than females. These communications were both positive and negative in quality. In the upper elementary grades, males received more academic feedback from teachers than did females. They also received more neutral, more non-academic, and more negative teacher feedback. The males were found to dominate the classrooms both in the positive sense as learners, as well as in a negative sense as behavioral problems.

Putnam and Self (1988) studied a group of preschool children with an average age of just under three years. Seven girls and eight boys made up the class. The results of their research indicated several interesting points regarding classroom interaction based on the gender of the students. The adults (all female)—a teacher, graduate assistants, and undergraduate student teachers—all interacted more frequently with the boys than the girls. These interactions also had a qualitative difference by gender. The teachers were found to be more likely to limit the behavioral choices of the boys than the girls, and the directives to the boys were more likely to be commands and corrections. The interactions with the girls more often took on the characteristics of distractions and requests. In this case, as in the research discussed earlier, the teachers interacted with the children based to some extent on the children's gender. These results may imply some previously conceived expectations on the adults' part about behaviors that boys may exhibit as opposed to behaviors that girls may exhibit. If a teacher chooses, consciously or unconsciously, to limit the options of one group of student, he or she has probably concluded that there is potential for negative behavior if the options are left more open. Unnecessary and inhibiting limits may be placed on the activities of boys simply because of their gender.

Teacher-initiated interactions, which are often rooted in gender stereotypes, can become particularly evident when examined within the context of a specific curricular area. This is especially true when the academic topic is one that traditionally has been considered either "masculine" or "feminine." A number of studies have been conducted that examine teacher interactions with students in the areas of math and science. In these two areas, one might expect distinct differences in how teachers interact with girls and with boys. Working from the accepted research results over an extended period that boys consistently score higher than girls in math, Fennema and Peterson (1987) were interested in exploring teacher-student interaction patterns to determine whether males interacted more than females with the teacher. Teachers of thirty-six fourth-grade math classes were studied. Some of the tasks asked of the students were categorized as being of low-level and some as being of high-level cognitive complexity. Fennema and Peterson discussed several interesting results. On both the low- and high-level cognitive complexity tasks, teachers were found to initiate more math related interactions with boys than girls. They also found that more non-volunteer interactions of a social nature were initiated by the teacher with boys, as well as more private social interactions with boys than girls. The authors of this study concluded that definite gender-based differences exist with regard to teacher-initiated interactions.

QUALITY OF INTERACTIONS

In addition to the issue of quantitative difference based on gender, there are some qualitative differences in how teachers interact with their students. This differentiation on the part of many teachers has to do with expectations, probably unconscious, that are largely based on the acceptance of gender stereotypes.

Qualitative differences of teacher interactions according to the gender of students is generally manifested through the intensity of academic interaction between teacher and student. Because higher-level questioning has been identified as a critical element in effective teaching and learning, much of the research in qualitative gender difference has been focused in that direction.

In a study that examined teacher responses to both discipline issues and pre-academic behavior by gender, Serbin et al. (1973) reported findings consistent with most of the similar research. Teachers were found to be more likely to respond to aggressively behaved boys than to girls who behaved similarly. They also used louder reprimands toward the boys than the girls. But also of interest were the findings that showed teachers were more likely to give direction and explicit instructions to the boys than to the girls when they sought help from them. In this study, teachers, probably unconsciously, provided more enabling instruction for boys than girls. Boys were likely to be told how to solve dilemmas, while girls were more likely to have the teacher provide the solution or do the task for them.

Less research exists that examines the quality of praise and criticism by gender than that regarding the quantity of it. Nonetheless, the findings of the following studies are pertinent for teachers considering gender equity in their classroom practice.

Dweck et al. (1978) found that praise initiated by the teacher that dealt with academic accomplishment differed by gender. After studying fourth- and fifth-grade students and their teachers, the researchers reported that roughly 90 percent of teachers' praise toward the boys concerned intellectual points. In comparison, about 80 percent of the praise the girls received similarly concerned intellectual quality of the accomplishment or task. The remaining praise toward the girls had to do with aspects of neatness or following the rules for the assignment. These subtle differences in quality of praise may give students messages that they assimilate over a period of time. Learners discover that the expectations of them are based to some degree on their gender rather than their individual needs or abilities. The students will tend to focus their efforts on those things that meet with the teacher's approval. In the case of this study, boys were reinforced for the academic quality of their work, while girls were praised less often for the quality and more often for the form of their work (Dweck et al. 1978).

Another interesting gender difference in quality of teacher-initiated interaction is in criticism of student work. Dweck and Gilliard (1975) found that the teachers they studied tended to criticize boys' poor performance on an academic task for lack of trying hard enough. This form of criticism was rarely found to be directed toward girls. Teachers tended to simply tell the girls that they had not done something correctly, while the boys received additional comments about their failure to try. The end result of these differences may be very different perceptions developed by girls as compared to boys regarding their levels of competence. When one is told that one can do better by trying harder, there is clearly hope provided for the student to accomplish more or succeed at a higher level. The student is quite likely to do better, because the means of doing so is laid out by the teacher. In the case of the criticism patterns of the teachers toward the girls, the girls do not receive the same nudge toward improved performance. They are simply told they have not done the task correctly. The implication is that girls are criticized more often for intellectual inadequacy, while boys are criticized more often for their lack of effort. Lack of effort is a problem much more easily fixed by the student than that of intellectual failing.

Good, Sikes, and Brophy (1973) chose sixteen junior-high teachers, both male and female, to study teacher interaction patterns with particular attention to qualitative differences according to the gender of the students. They found that in general boys received more attention from the teacher, despite the gender of the teacher. The higher achieving boys received the most positive interactions with the teachers. Boys who were considered to be lower achieving also received attention from teachers. However, the tone of the interactions was generally negative. These boys were likely to receive criticism and less feedback about their academic work. The researchers also concluded that more questions of a process nature were asked of boys, while the questions asked most often of the girls were product-based. In other words, the boys were more likely to be asked to respond to questions that required higher-level thinking skills than were girls.

In considering the preceding research, there is a strong tendency to deny the possibility that teacher practices, which when listed as above appear very obvious and overt, could possibly be occurring in modern classrooms. The fact that these gender-differentiated teacher interactions are quite commonplace attests to the power of the subtle gender bias most of us continue to hold. While young students do not as a rule articulate gender-specific teacher expectations (the teacher expects certain things from boys and other things from girls), older students do. They may do this through curriculum choice (general science rather than physics) or through casual comments about their comfort level in a particular content area. Because nearly all teachers interact with their students in a gender-biased fashion to some degree, students may come to understand that expectations of them are based in part on their gender. As with any kind of bias being practiced, the outcome for students is that opportunities may be limited.

Simply knowing that gender-biased teaching practices are harmful to students is not sufficient to enable one to avoid them. Glimpses into the classrooms of Judy, Karen, Mary, Sean, and Beth help illustrate how these teachers choose to implement aspects of gender equity in their teaching through the context of teacher-initiated interactions. As you will note, there are some commonalities among the teachers, despite the various ages of their students. There are also some distinct differences among the teachers, both in their interpretations of gender equity and their views of themselves in relationship to their students.

Because a teacher's general approach to students is often dictated in large part by the age or developmental stage of the students, it may be helpful to examine by chronological order of the students' grade how these teachers structure their interactions as they incorporate gender equity. A preschool teacher is more likely to touch his or her students and become physically involved in their learning activities, while a high-school teacher is more likely to interact with her or his students in a group, being less personally involved in each student's classroom activities. While some of the differences in approach logically can be explained through the developmental needs of students at different stages, the different interpretation of teacher contact can also be explained by tradition or convention. Teachers of older students tend to perceive their role as teaching content, rather than teaching students. The former view of the teacher's role enables the teacher of secondary students to be fairly disassociated from the students on a personal level. So it is logical to assume that certain methods of achieving gender equity that a third-grade teacher might use would be awkward at best in a high-school biology class. In order to provide a broad basis within which the reader can consider different approaches to gender equity through teacher-initiated interactions, a variety of classroom settings and situations follow.

THE TEACHERS' INTERACTIONS

Judy's Preschool Class

Judy's equality-based interactions with her students illustrate her considered attempt to work with each student as an individual, yet carefully allocate equal quantity and quality of her attention to each child.

The day begins at 9:00. The five boys and eight girls all have arrived by 9:20, each accompanied by their mothers. The children are in mixed-age classes, with three-, four-, and five-year-olds together. Of the fourteen children enrolled in Judy's class, two are special-needs students, both girls. Judy greets each of the children in the same fashion, if not with identical words. Boys and girls are spoken to in an adult tone of voice, reminded to stow their belongings in their cubbies. Even though two of the girls appear in designer outfits and another girl wears a frilly dress complete with party shoes, Judy does not comment on their appearance. Instead she remarks about their facial expressions and readiness for the day.

> "It's good to see you this morning. I like the way you look ready to get started."

Judy intentionally keeps her praise gender neutral and steers away from commenting about physical appearance. She remarks:

> Girls are too often complimented about their appearance rather than their ability. I don't comment about the girls' pretty clothes or hair.

She encourages each student to become engaged in any activity at one of the five centers set up around the room.

The students initially are not steered to a particular center. They may go where they like. Judy moves continuously from child to child. She interacts with each, squatting down to her or his eye level as she speaks with each child. After she briefly has worked with each child, she begins her rounds again, taking care that she speaks with each again.

In monitoring the students, she is careful about interacting with all the children equally. As they work, each child receives exactly the same amount of teacher interaction as the next. The quantity of academic interaction time (or in the case of preschool, center activity work) is intentionally doled out in equal amounts. Judy also is conscious of equalizing the content, or quality, of her interactions. As she engages each student in discussions and descriptions of her or his activities, she displays no preconceived notions about gender-based interests or abilities. The content of the discussion she holds with several girls in the home center is quite similar to the content of a later discussion with a boy playing in this center.

One interesting center contains small dishes of brown and black paint, with containers of marbles. The purpose of the activity is to provide several different tactile sensations as the child rolls marbles in the gooey paint. The colors of brown and black are intentionally chosen. Judy explains that by using these colors she is sending a subtle message to the children that these are good colors. During conversations with children at this center she talks about the richness of the brown and black. She believes that, at some level, the children may make the transference of these paint colors being good to those skin colors being good, as well. Judy does not dole out effusive praise or encouragement. Instead, she engages each child in a discussion about what she or he is doing:

> "John, I see you are interested in rolling the marbles in the brown paint. Describe for me what that feels like. What an interesting design you've made. What does it look like to you?"

Later in the morning, Elizabeth sits at this center. The conversation between Judy and Elizabeth is almost exactly the same as the earlier one with John.

Several important issues are being addressed in these interactions. Because her students are young, just beginning to develop ideas of what school might be like and what it means to do work, constant monitoring by Judy is essential. Because of the developmental needs of the students, language development also is a primary goal of the program. In addressing these two needs, Judy frames her monitoring and interactions in the context of verbal exploration with the children. Her verbal interactions tend not to be in the form of statements, but rather questions. Obviously, she is interested in pressing the children to expand their thinking and the verbal description of those thoughts. As she is pursuing these goals, she does so in the context of gender equity. She monitors herself so that the number and quality of the interactions are equal for girls and boys. In this respect Judy's approach could be described as very gender neutral, which reflects her understanding of gender equity based on a framework of equality. Her interpretation of gender equity is one where girls and boys should and do receive equal quantity and quality of academic interactions.

Judy's academic goals for the students require her to be exceedingly neutral and equal in her attention. In fact, one is struck by the calm and settled tone of the class. Even as minor disruptions occur, Judy addresses the children involved in the situations in a matter-of-fact way, encouraging them to think through the solution to their conflict.

And the disruptions do occur. Further, the conflicts in which the children become enmeshed are strikingly different by gender. The boys argue over game rules and territory, while the girls zero in on personality issues. Another obvious difference is the aggressiveness of some of the boys compared to the girls, who are all fairly quiet and non-aggressive physically. In fact, the behavior patterns of these three-, four-, and five-year-olds are quite consistent with gender stereotypes. Because the boys in Judy's class are the ones who act out and in general tend to be the behavior problems, it would be natural for her to direct a large part of her non-academic attention to the boys. Judy agrees that the boys in her class require more redirection than the girls. This is a point she has reflected upon within the context of gender equity. She discusses the influence of early socialization in the home:

> I think that the boys are getting more mixed messages. Expectations for girls are to be low-keyed, and to speak in quiet voices. All those kinds of things are pretty consistent between home and school. I think boys are given more leeway at home, and what is considered to be aggressive when you put fourteen kids in a room, just seems boyish when there are one or two kids at home. I find children are less tolerant of aggression on the part of boys, regardless of their gender. It somehow feels more threatening when a boy aggresses than when a girl does.

When asked whether she feels she spends more time with one gender of student than the other, she acknowledges that because the boys tend to misbehave more often than the girls, she deals with the boys more often.

> I think this year I have more boys with discipline issues than girls. So my job becomes not being the disciplinarian but the teacher. So that I have a contact with those boys when it's not about discipline, and just because they're misbehaving, it doesn't mean they get all of my attention. I just have to save a lot of pieces of me.

Consistent with Judy's interpretation of gender equity, she is very conscious of giving the boys in her class, who more often misbehave, positive attention in addition to redirection of their negative behavior. She constantly monitors herself to insure that the boys do not receive the bulk of the attention, and that the attention that they do receive is not primarily negative in tone and content.

> I think about this issue. After the children leave for day, I think back to how I've acted with the boys and the girls, to be sure everyone gets the same amount of attention, but that the boys don't get only negative attention.

A situation that occurred in the home center illustrates how Judy carries out this careful balance. As described in chapter 3, the home center contains a cabinet with dishes, a table and chairs, dress-up clothes, and a variety of baby dolls. Judy has paid careful attention to furnishing the area. The dress-up clothes include a variety of male and female clothes. Sequined gowns, aprons, construction hard-hats, men's work shirts, and a variety of men's and women's shoes are available for the children to try on. The babies are black, white, brown, and Asian. All are anatomically correct; three are female and one is male. Two girls finished playing "house," setting the table for a meal and cradling their babies. They took off their aprons and left the center for another activity. The two oldest and largest boys entered the area. After rummaging through the dress-up clothes and choosing large men's shirts to wear, they turned to the baby dolls. Each boy picked up one and began to shake and shout at the dolls. The noise level began to escalate as the boys became increasingly more violent in their "play" with the dolls, culminating with their stabbing, punching, and throwing the dolls against the wall. Despite the noise level, the other children scattered about the room paid no attention to the boys. Judy calmly turned to the boys, asking them not to play so rough. She followed this directive with the question, "How can you play in the center more quietly?" The boys' reaction to the redirection was to put the dolls aside. They turned to the chairs in the area, placed them front to back, and began to play "train."

Clearly, another teacher might have acted differently, but Judy's interpretation of the incident and her actions toward the boys are consistent with her concern about her interactions and not dealing with boys only on a punitive basis. The classroom rule of being quiet enough so that others can play uninterrupted was enforced without a lecture about how to nurture or care for babies. She clearly wanted to allow the boys to play with the dolls as they wished without infusing her particular values about what appropriate interactions with babies might entail.

A final method, which is central to the way Judy conceives of gender equity, is that of discussing different points of view with the children. While the results of thinking through two diverse points of view might not become evident in the child's behavior on the spot, Judy believes that if cognitive conflict or dissonance is created for the child, the child will eventually work toward a better understanding of an idea or situation. In her interactions with the children that have a direct bearing on an issue of gender equity, this is the primary approach she uses. She illustrates her understanding of cognitive conflict regarding gender equity through this story previously mentioned in chapter 3:

> There are times when a child will bring in a book with very sex-
> ist images in it. We will talk about "Is this your experience?"
> One girl's mother is a physician. Yet when a book showed a
> woman in that role, the girl said women can't be doctors.
> There's nothing in her background that says that, except the
> messages in society.

Rather than telling the girl she has made an inaccurate statement,
Judy prefers to prod the child into thinking about what she has
experienced and how that experience fits with her statement. Even
when the child ends the discussion with, "Women just aren't doctors," Judy feels confident that the child eventually will come to
understand the obvious discrepancy between her experience and
her statement.

An incident in the classroom provided another example of
Judy's approach to questioning and creating cognitive conflict.
Kevin retrieved a cowboy hat from the home center and went to
the area where two saddles rested on a beam. He mounted the
saddle and became a cowboy. Sarah began to mount the other
saddle. Kevin immediately became hostile, saying: "You can't ride
with me. Girls can't be cowboys."

Judy was within earshot and immediately walked over to
Kevin. Kevin had broken a classroom rule that no one can be
excluded from an activity. Rather than reminding Kevin of the
rule, Judy chose to discuss with Kevin his rationale for attempting
to exclude Sarah. She began by asking why Sarah couldn't ride
with him. Kevin reported that she just couldn't, that girls were
different. Judy asked Kevin,

> "How is it girls are different from boys?" Kevin responded,
> "Well, they just are. They look different. Their hair is different,
> their faces are different, their teeth are different and stuff."

Judy continued to talk with Kevin, structuring most of her part of
the discussion in the form of questions. She continued to press
him about how, other than length of hair (she did note that his
hair was longer than some of the girls in the room), he concluded
that girls were so different that Sarah should not ride the saddle
next to his. There was no dramatic conclusion to their interaction. Kevin did not articulate an opinion about why he might or
might not suggest exclusion solely based on gender. And Judy did
not insist that he do so. Rather than be frustrated or annoyed
about Kevin's obvious sexist attitudes, as expressed by his reluc-

tance to play with a girl, Judy was satisfied that Kevin mentally would replay the discussion later, and that he might begin to rethink his exclusionary policy when it comes to gender. Judy succinctly describes her method as follows:

> I'm not interested in having children learn propaganda lines, so they know the "right" answer, as in putting them into a state of cognitive conflict. I'll leave things in the air, just knowing I've created a question in that child's mind that they've got to work with. Maybe they won't agree with me, but if they keep getting contradictory messages and these mount up, they'll be ready to look at that notion and see it doesn't fit anymore.

Judy's interactions subtly create questions in the minds of the children. She believes these questions will resurface at a later time for the children and provide meaning for them in redirecting their thinking about gender stereotypes. Her means of structuring these interactions allows for teacher-student communication that is indirect and non-confrontational. Her interactions also are based on the idea of strict neutrality in dealing with girls and boys; on the basis of equal treatment, rather than equitable treatment.

Karen's Kindergarten

Karen's kindergarten is a place where gender equity is discussed from the beginning of the school year. Although Karen and Judy share many of the same concerns about gender equity, an examination of their interactions with students reveal some differences. Karen believes in confronting issues and discussing them directly. Because she considers gender equity the most critical and powerful issue having to do with human interaction, she spends considerable time and energy in addressing it. However, when asked if she structures her classroom in a particular way to meet gender equity goals, she stresses she does not.

> If you walked in you wouldn't say this is a room that deals with gender equity. But when I'm challenging children about where to work, that's where that comes in. I'm not trying to teach them equity, I'm trying to assist them in living equitably.

One is struck by the independence and capability of the students in Karen's class. As in Judy's class of slightly younger children, a primary goal is to guide the learners toward independent work skills as well as problem-solving capabilities. The latter is particularly focused on social interactions. Both in the play centers such as the block area or the home center, as well as the more academically-oriented centers such as reading or math, the children work quietly but often collaboratively on the assignments. One clear difference between the preschool class and this kindergarten class is the emphasis in the kindergarten on group work. While Judy's learners tend to operate separately or in pairs, Karen's students work on activities in larger groups of five or six students. During the center time, Karen and the classroom aide each locate themselves in an academic center. The other two groups not with the teacher or the aide work independently. This of course is common practice in kindergartens. What is impressive and different here is the lack of conflict among the children within the groups. They are task-oriented and quite companionable.

The students' day begins with the entire K-3 school meeting in the courtyard for the community pledge. The principal announces new items. It is Karen's class's turn to conduct the Pledge of Allegiance. One of the girls in her class leads the school in reciting it. Following the pledge, the guests visiting the school that day are introduced to the children and the teachers. The principal wishes them all a good day, and the children head to their classroom. A strong sense of community and esprit de corps exists. This sense of unity carries over into Karen's classroom. As the children enter the classroom, Karen directs them to the discussion corner, where the children seat themselves in a circle. After they are settled, Karen says, "I like how you have mixed yourselves on the rug." One boy offers, "Hey, it's girl/boy, girl/boy." Karen reinforces this by saying: "Yes, I like that." She then moves on to discuss the coming day's activities.

From the beginning of the school year, a frequent topic of classroom discussion has been that of getting to know other people who may be different than you are. While ethnicity and neighborhood affiliation are aspects of the discussion, gender is a principal part, too. In achieving her goal of helping her learners become equitable in their living styles, she openly addresses issues of gender stereotyping that may inhibit the children from mixing and freely learning together.

Throughout the morning's activities, when the children are allowed to choose their own activities, Karen monitors each child often. She moves from one activity center to another, interacting with each child. She is warm without being effusive. In contrast to

Judy's strikingly neutral and equal fashion of interaction with regard to gender, Karen's interactions are far less uniform among students. The content and direction of her interactions seem more to be based more on the individual child's academic and social development.

Kelsey, the most precocious reader of the group, is described by Karen as being bossy, pushy, and in general intolerant of many of the other students. As Kelsey is committing one of her many social blunders (in this case, telling another student that he is a terrible reader), Karen reprimands Kelsey for her insensitivity. This is Kelsey's principal weakness, and Karen addresses it directly and critically. One suspects that if another student were to have done the same thing, and it was clearly not a primary concern for that child, Karen would have dealt with that child quite differently. Rather than equalize interactions with each student, Karen is more interested in addressing the issues that concern that child.

While a part of Karen's interpretation of gender equity dictates that she structure her interactions with children on an equal basis, and the quantity of Karen's interactions by gender is quite even as evidenced by her constant monitoring of all children on a somewhat rotating basis, the quality or the content of the interactions stems from an equity interpretation. The words and actions she uses toward each child are the result of Karen's belief in the power of gender role stereotyping and her assumption that many children fall victim to it. The group she has identified as at-risk are girls and boys who exhibit a strong tendency toward gender-based stereotyped behavior and attitudes. Girls who will not enter the block area and boys who will not participate in the home center are the focus of Karen's attention, sometimes to the partial exclusion of the children who demonstrate skills and interests in all of the curricular areas. Children less needy, in Karen's view, of equity intervention may receive a lesser quantity of her attention and a different quality of interaction. Karen's interactions with the kindergartners are the result of an interpretation of gender equity as both an equality and an equitable issue.

Karen sees the behavior of many of the girls and boys in her class as a result of home and general societal socialization that have gone far to reinforce gender stereotyping in her learners. When asked about discipline issues differing along gender lines, she acknowledges that girls and boys often misbehave differently in her class.

I don't think it's innate that boys are more acting out and girls tend to be more manipulative and helpless. Girls seem to be helpless in how to solve the problem, and boys in knowing other ways in how to solve the problem. But then you get the exception to the rule, the girl who knocks them down, and is real physical, and the boy who cries to have you take care of him.

Because Karen believes that there are real differences in typical girl behavior and typical boy behavior, she approaches her interactions with the students with this in mind. She focuses her attention on helping girls become independent in finding solutions to problems and on helping boys discover solutions to problems that do not require physical means. To that end, she focuses on remedying limitations that result from gender-role stereotyping for both sexes. She also, however, is watchful for the boys who need to develop more independent skills and girls who need to develop problem-solving skills of a verbal rather than physical nature.

Judy and Karen both have a strong commitment to dealing with gender equity in their classrooms. However, their approaches to the issue differ, creating differences in the structure and content of their interactions with their students. For Karen, gender issues are areas to be directly addressed and confronted. She believes that the preconceived gender stereotypes with which her students come to her are biases that must be addressed by her in the classroom and within the context of the school day. She goes about redressing gender biases in the children on an individual basis. If a girl falls into the stereotypical pattern of learned helplessness, Karen directly addresses that behavior for that child. Similarly, if a boy also demonstrates that problem, Karen will address it. However, because she is concerned with redirecting behavior patterns and attitudes of children that are reflections of gender stereotypes, her interactions with girls will vary from those with boys in confronting a given problem. While she is not focused exclusively on dealing with stereotypical behaviors, she is very conscious of them and deals with them directly.

Mary's Third Grade

The eight- and nine-year-olds in Mary's third-grade class are quite different developmentally from Judy's preschoolers and Karen's kindergartners. The curriculum and, to some extent, the teacher's interactions with her students are guided by the heavier emphasis on academic learning rather than the socially focused learning in the earlier grades. While she is conscious of equal treatment of her students by gender, she also demonstrates her sense of a need to assert the role of females, in social studies for example, and to consciously work toward the empowerment of the girls in her class. She actively addresses gender equity in ways similar to Karen.

To a great extent, Mary's personal experiences have directed her concern toward gender issues in the classroom. Having experienced a number of situations where her gender rendered her less powerful than a male would have been in the same circumstances, she indicates determination that the girls she works with will be more empowered as females than she was as a younger person.

> I want girls to know about women who could be heroes to them. I want them to know that women can be adventurous and courageous, that they weren't just these compassionate, caring little things. Those are all wonderful virtues. Those are certainly all valuable but aren't determined by gender. We all have a little of those things. I want kids to know that. I want them to leave school real proud and capable.

Mary is conscious of wanting to empower the girls in her class, but she also discusses the need for providing a gender balance in her interactions with her students.

In a fashion somewhat similar to Karen's, Mary has set ground rules from the beginning of the school year. Her approach to dealing with gender equity includes open discussion and directness.

> There is a rule that you don't deny playing to anyone for any reason. We did have to talk about it. They're really into boys against girls. When we have a class soccer game, we don't do boys against girls. And we don't line up that way. At the beginning of the year, I had to teach that. I was real clear about not wanting them to line up that way or to in any way deny that we were all one class. And we had done a lot about rights and responsibilities, or had begun to do it at that time. We have a list of class rights and what our responsibilities are and to meet those rights. Those are the same for everybody in here. And it didn't matter if you were a boy or a girl. I told them it bothered me to see people separated and throughout the year they would work with boys and girls, and that we needed to all be one. I

also said that we wouldn't leave the room unless it was mixed, so it was mixed.

Mary's students, thirteen boys and nine girls, enter the classroom after lunch at 12:55. The students move to a reading area, which is furnished with a loft, a rug, several large pillows, and one wooden fence rail. Mary and the students settle down for a story-reading session that is connected to a social studies unit about pioneers settling the western United States.

> Mary introduces the readings by saying, "These are women's diary entries." A boy seated not far from the teacher groans. Mary responds with, "Do you have a problem?" Another boy says, "He doesn't like girls." Mary responds with, "Sure he does."

Mary chooses neither a strong confrontational method with the boy, nor does she choose to ignore the incident.

A number of the students leave the room for math instruction with a different teacher, while a number of other students enter. Part of Mary's role is to provide math instruction for the third-grade students who are considered more advanced in their achievement. The boys and girls in the class are excited and energized. As Mary questions them, she is careful to alternate by gender. A tally taken during the math lesson indicates that every student is called on once.

During two other math sessions, as well as instructional sessions with her regular class in other topics, the tallies indicate similar results. Mary takes care to address the issue of quantity of time allocated to her female and male students through her questioning and oral assessment of their knowledge. However, she also is conscious that in some ways some of the boys may be getting more of her time during the day. When asked if she considered either boys or girls to be more of a discipline problem than the other, she responded that some of the boys tended to be more of a disciplinary problem than the girls, during this academic year, anyway. Further, she believes that the behavioral problems tend to be gender differentiated. Her interpretation is quite similar to Karen's.

> I think there are different kinds of trouble. I'm sorry to say that, but there really are. With the boys it's more often physical and an inability to control anger, or to get what they want without reverting to shoving, pushing, or raising their voices. They're

more likely to act out—tip the chair back, tip the desk. With the girls it's apt to be too much socializing, over-dependence on a partner, hurt feelings over something that happened at break.

Resolving the boys' behavior problems tends to interrupt the class time, while the girls' problems are more often dealt with quietly and privately in a conference situation. Mary perceives a difference in misbehavior as a gender equity issue. She is aware that the boys in her class this year may be receiving more negative attention from her than the girls. Although she does not compensate for this inequity in the same fashion as Judy, she is conscious of the problem and attempts to mediate the difference through disciplinary actions that are fairly subtle and unobtrusive whenever possible. A quiet word to or a hand on the shoulder of a student are some means she uses to minimize the interruption of instruction and to lessen the amount of negative attention paid to boys in particular.

A final point about quantity of interactions by gender is the possible difference in who creates more learning opportunities for themselves. Mary perceives that, in this particular class, there is no difference in learning opportunity by gender. When asked if girls or boys seem to dominate the class or in general talk out more, she described the dynamics this way:

> I've got some of each who do that. My two biggest talkers with the most ideas are girls. But I've got a lot of boys who are the same way. If I start out on something, no matter what it is, I have two girls that are going to be right on it. They're going to have their hand up, and they're going to want to volunteer. They're going to be real aggressive about making their ideas known. I also have my boys who want to be heard, who always have an idea that's very creative. So there's a balance.

The possible domination of one group over another by co-opting her time is something Mary also is conscious of. In this particular class make-up, she does not believe that one gender of student tends to dominate, although it is clear that certain individuals do. She addresses this through careful monitoring of each student and inclusion of all students on an equal basis through her questioning and other interactions. As illustrated earlier, Mary takes up gender issues primarily through her use of particular materials and curriculum adaptation. But she also is conscientious about doling out her attention to students in an equal way.

When students bring up gender issues, as in the case of the boy who was unhappy about the readings from the women's diaries, Mary gently but directly addresses the point. Regarding her interactions with students in the form of monitoring and questioning, she integrates her understanding of gender equity by giving equal attention to all students.

Sean's Middle-School Art Classes

Sean has been teaching middle school art for twenty-one of his thirty-one years of teaching. He exudes energy and interest in his students and his work. When asked how he thinks about gender equity in his teaching practice, he describes a concern about the individual, within which gender issues lie. He is aware of cultural or ethnic considerations, special needs of the students who are mainstreamed into his classes, as well as gender concerns. In discussing his interpretation of gender equity specifically and the means by which he incorporates it into his teaching, Sean describes his efforts as focused through his approach to classroom management and interactions with his students:

> I think I'm more likely to think of it in terms of classroom management. I think the students in the classroom are pretty well balanced as to where the attention is going. That is, I may have a class where I have one or two girls I have to think about. Where am I going to move them so they can be more involved in the activity and less of a distraction? In the next class it may be a couple of boys. If the class is not running well, I am inclined to take a look at the way I am approaching and structuring it more than I am to say, "Oh, this class is terrible." I don't think it's really the class, it's more what I'm doing about it.

Sean is very conscious of the control he can exert in creating an effective classroom in which he can treat his students equally.

Observation of Sean's seventh- and eight-grade art classes reveal his commitment to include all students in the activities of the class, as well as his interpretation of gender equity as an issue of equal treatment for both genders. The eleven boys and twelve girls in the fourth period seventh-grade art class enter with a wave of energy and noise. They find their folders at a particular station in the room, depending on the extent to which they have progressed on the assignment. The bell rings, and Sean calls the class to attention. The initial four minutes of the class are given over to instruction of new material. The next project will be to create papier-maché masks. Sean centers himself in the large classroom so that all students can see the demonstration. All listen. Sean talks through each step of the demonstration, then asks for any questions. None are forthcoming. Sean then directs the students to begin; either to finish their current project or to begin the new one. The students open their folders amid quiet conversation, and Sean begins monitoring them. Sean radiates energy, moving from student to student, critically examining the work. For the next thirty-five minutes of the class period, Sean is in constant motion, making his way around the classroom, then making the rounds again. He interacts with each student. His attention to their progress regarding the class work is distributed to the students on an equal basis.

As was the case in Judy's preschool class, one is struck with the even and equal quality of the interactions in addition to the equal quantity. Praise and criticism are given without regard to gender; the words used are almost exactly the same for each student. Further, for those students seeking help, his response is identical. None of the students is told exactly how to carry out a task; rather Sean asks them questions about how they think the solution to their problem can be found. A boy calls out for help: "How come this stuff isn't sticking?" Sean asks the boy to review the steps demonstrated earlier in the making of the papier maché. In doing so, the boy realizes he has missed a step. Sean leaves to resume his monitoring as the boy starts over. As Sean approaches one of the girls, she asks a different question about the consistency of the papier maché. In responding to her Sean repeats, word for word, his questioning as he had done with the male student. The girl repeats the steps in the making of papier maché, and she, too, discovers her error. Sean goes on to the next group of students as this girl begins again. Throughout this class period, as well as the other nine class sessions observed, Sean carefully attends to each student on a very equal basis. The quality of these interactions also is strictly equal. Sean's academic expectations for his students are the same; students are required to solve their own problems and stay on task.

As has been the case with the other teachers discussed, Sean also perceives a difference by gender with regard to misbehavior. In general, Sean believes that boys tend to present more disciplinary problems than girls.

I think boys are more of a discipline problem. I'm more likely to take a boy to the office than I am a girl. I don't take a lot of people to the office, but the last ten times I've taken someone, it's been a boy. The difference is that a boy, especially in middle school, really tests the limits. Most girls understand "This is the end. I don't want you to do this again," and they won't. Boys will push one more time more frequently.

Sean believes the difference in general behavior patterns is due to socialization, with society giving messages about how males and females should or should not act. And he is conscious of the fact that males may be dealt with more often in the area of punishment than girls.

This aspect of Sean's classroom management clearly is neither equal nor equitable. However, in order to keep the classroom control that he feels is necessary in these very heterogeneous elective classes, he acts quickly at the beginning of any misbehavior. In a sense, he takes as a given that socialized gender differences exist. In order for his students to experience success in the art classes, he feels he must maintain control and keep them on task. Even though the male students are affected by the "trips to the office" on a disparate basis, he is willing to overlook this inequity in order to meet the goal of order and completion of task.

While Sean does not press his students to finish projects from a subject-matter driven perspective, as do many of his middle school and high school colleagues, he does associate completion of work with higher self-esteem and student satisfaction. With careful regard to equity in the form of respect for individual differences and needs, Sean carefully allots his time and attention to each student on an equal basis, while tolerating no deviant behavior, which he believes is more likely to come from his male students than female students.

Beth's Middle-School Science Classes

Beth teaches seventh- and eighth-grade science. Like Mary, she is committed to enhancing the opportunities of her female students and, like Karen, she perceives gender equity as the primary lens through which she focuses her teaching. Without question, Beth is an assertive and proactive feminist. Her interpretation of gender equity is equitable rather than equal, and her approach in both the classroom and school in general might be considered by some as radical. Beth interprets the situation in which she teaches as one where aggressive means are required in order to better empower the girls and, to a lesser extent, the boys. However, in order to empower the boys, she believes the girls must be given particular and unequal opportunities. As the girls grow and profit from these opportunities, the boys will eventually be able to enter into relationships with them that will be more equal and less susceptible to problems such as family violence. Beth's students are principally Hispanic and Native American, from low-income homes. Through her personal relationships with her students she has become aware of a high rate of physical abuse, sexual abuse, and family violence. She believes that through the personal empowerment of her female students, these life styles can be altered for the coming generation. Therefore she accentuates the opportunities for the girls, but at the same time does not ignore the boys. The high engagement rate in her classes is a tribute to her skill as a teacher, but also a reflection of her commitment to involving girls in a content area that is traditionally considered "masculine." The girls' participation and achievement in the class is as strong as that of the boys. However, this equality of outcome is present, in Beth's opinion, only because of the extra attention and focus on the girls.

Beth begins the school year conscious that boys and girls will likely react to her differently and along gender lines. She says,

> At the beginning of the year, the boys love me. I'm funny, charismatic, a jock, and have sports stories. So they can share some of that stuff. But by the second or third quarter, the girls have picked up that I listen, which the girls like. And the boys like that, too—that I really care about them. The girls succeed in my class, and they're not used to succeeding in science. I have so many girls who say, "Oh my God, I've always hated science." I definitely share with the girls what they like to talk about. We like to talk about our families, boyfriends, friends. It's all very open.

Beth sees that many of her students' interests are shaped by fairly rigid gender role expectations, particularly in these cultures, where there is apt to be strong distinction between gender roles. Based on that interpretation, she structures her informal and casual interactions with her students so that males and females feel they have an affiliation within the environment of the classroom.

While she clearly believes that the boys in her classes require attention and empowerment as learners, she does not believe that resources (in this case, her attention) should be equally divided along gender lines. This becomes evident when observing her teaching.

The bell rings at 10:15, which marks the beginning of Beth's second period eighth-grade science class. Beth says, "All right folks, we will begin."

One female student is not seated. Beth writes her name on the blackboard in the corner and proceeds with a short introduction to the content and activities for the day. The girl whose name is on the board notices it, says nothing and shows no change in expression, finds her seat and turns her attention to Beth, as have all the other students. Beth displays momentum and energy. She goes through the introduction to acid rain without a pause. The students all have their eyes trained on her. Following the introduction, Beth begins to ask review questions. "Where does acid rain come from?" she asks.

A boy seated in the back shouts out an answer. Beth studiously ignores him and calls on a girl seated in the front left who does not have her hand raised.

"Sonya, where does acid rain come from?' she asks.

The girl promptly answers correctly. Another question is put forth. Boys' and girls' hands go up. Beth calls on a girl with her hand raised, whose response to the question is only partially correct.

"That's only part of the answer. What else can you add?" Beth asks Maria.

Hands wave, but Beth waits a full fifteen seconds until Maria adds additional information to her answer. More questions follow. During this time Beth calls on boys, but the frequency by gender is not equal. In fact, she calls on about twice the number of girls than boys, many of whom have not volunteered to answer. When answers are given by either boys or girls that are not correct or complete, she directly tells the student so and waits until that student completes the answer. Through this style of questioning Beth is incorporating aspects of her philosophy of gender equity, as well as displaying effective teaching strategies.

In her commitment to empower girls, she does not evenly distribute her resources. More girls are called on than are boys. Further, she does not restrict her solicitation for answers from willing volunteers. She calls on girls who do not have hands raised. She is confident that they can do the work and get the right answers, and this expectation is relayed to the girls. Each one called on does know the answer and has proven her success in science to herself and the rest of the group. Several times, boys shouted out answers without waiting to be called on. While Beth may have ignored girls doing the same thing, it is only the boys who engage in this means of attention getting. By ignoring them, Beth is controlling the issue of dominance in the class. In this case, the girls dominate slightly because Beth calls on them more. But this is a conscious effort on her part, consistent with her view of gender issues.

While Beth intentionally overemphasizes the participation of the girls in her class through more frequent questioning, her monitoring activities demonstrate a far more even distribution by gender. Throughout the portion of the class during which the students are engaged in the lab, Beth walks among the students. She speaks to and checks on the progress of each student on a rotating basis. As students have questions, Beth moves to that cluster of students, but goes back to the area of the room where she was before answering the question. From that point she proceeds with her monitoring activities. Beth's constant movement through the class keeps the students on task and helps maintain the momentum of the lesson. Her pattern of monitoring indicates a very equal distribution of her attention so that all of the students will complete the assignment.

As she is very equal in her monitoring, there is evidence that she also approaches discipline so that it is clear that certain behaviors, whether produced by a girl or a boy, will have the same consequences. Beth's classroom is distinguished by a distinct climate. She is casual and friendly with the students. She knows them all well and asks many questions about their lives before class begins. The students call her by her first name. When class begins, she assumes control. Several things are clear: She has made the rules clear from the beginning, and when infractions of those rules occur she follows through with the consequences that she said she would. For her, the use of assertive discipline is effective. Student names go on the board if they are even slightly disruptive. Beth does this without interrupting her progression through the lesson. Due largely to her consistency in administering her disciplinary program, as well as other aspects of her skill in teaching, there are very few class disruptions. These few tend to be whispering to a neighbor, failure to be ready for class to begin, or getting off task. The checks administered to students are quite even by gender. Following each of the ten classes observed, the tally on the board revealed that, proportionately, girls received as many checks as boys.

Although Beth expects the same appropriate behaviors from both genders and does not ignore some behaviors if they are committed by a student of a particular gender group, she does perceive that general behavior patterns differ by gender. When asked if she feels that boys or girls are more likely to be behavioral problems in her class, she answered this way:

> The truth is, in my 3½ years of teaching in this district, of the kids you wish weren't in your class, those kids are boys. The boys are less able to keep their hands off other kids. There are boys who are tough. That's really the only behavioral problem that's really hard for me. Most kids really like my class, so sitting in isolation one day, they want to be back. I've done that five times a year. I definitely give boys detention more often. I don't think boys get their names on the board more often than girls. Girls have more complete discipline, so they can control it if they don't want to get another check. Girls get checks for talking, or writing notes. That's something it's easier to have more self-discipline about. Girls don't tend to interrupt me as much, either.

While Beth perceives a gender difference in the types of misbehavior that may occur in the class, she is conscious of calling any student on her or his offense. Because note writing as well as loudly disrupting the class both come under the heading of not being on task, the tally by gender of names on the board at the end of a class period does represent both genders proportionately.

In a sense, Beth does not particularly care about the gender differentiation of classroom misbehavior. She cares most deeply about the motivation of her students and their success in the class. Consistent with her perspective of gender equity, she is most troubled when her female students are apathetic and non-participatory. She believes the girls to be more at risk for not achieving in science than the boys, who are more likely to be more comfortable in a course that middle-school students themselves describe as "masculine."

Some girls drive me nuts in a deeper way, because they're not motivated. These girls I consider kids that just aren't there. If my class doesn't inherently motivate you, something is really wrong. Something is wrong at home. So I worry about them. I want to shake them, and say This is your life. I don't take it personally, but it's a deeper worry.

Beth's interpretation of gender equity dictates much of her teaching strategy and her interactions with her students. It is clear from observing her over time that her students are drawn to her. This is due in part to a combination of her personality and skills as a teacher, which allow for a classroom climate that is simultaneously casual and in control, as well as her willingness to become involved in her students' lives by knowing their interests and troubles. These interaction strategies enable both male and female students to feel cared for and encouraged in this middle-school science class. But because Beth fiercely believes that the girls in her classes are more at risk in motivation and achievement in school, and ultimately at greater risk for leading lives that they do not feel empowered to control, she directs more of her energy toward them. When asked about the distribution of resources in her class—her time and attention specifically, she replied that all students should receive as much teaching as possible. However, when the question was presented in the context of there being a limited supply of these valuable teacher commodities, she said, "I think it's OK to exclude any majority group to give the minority group a voice; to empower them that they have a voice."

While Beth does not operationalize this point of view to the extent that her male students are ignored, she does intentionally give females more attention. In a very real sense, Beth sees this pattern as an act of compensation for what she believes is the common experience of her female students in their other classes. Although she works to involve her colleagues in gender equitable practices, only a few share her interests and particular concerns about girls. Because gender equity tends to be ignored or denied by the bulk of her colleagues, she believes that, in general, her female students do not have equal opportunities to learn and achieve in many of their other classes. Her class becomes one of the few where the girls feel particularly empowered and successful. Her interactions are unequal by gender, yet when viewed within the context of the entire school experience for the academic year, Beth believes her overcompensation may help to balance the sense of success for the girls to become more equal to that of the boys.

SUMMARY

Understanding teacher-initiated interactions is important with regard to general issues affecting effective teaching, and particularly in relationship to gender equity practiced in the classroom. Through careful consideration of one's questioning and monitoring practices, as well as disciplinary practices, the teacher can create an environment where gender-equity goals may be realized and where female and male students can all become empowered learners.

A sampling of the research illustrates how classrooms are often places where male students tend to dominate the interactions and the classroom at large. The domination is both quantitative and qualitative. While this domination may be quite unintentional on the part of the students as well as the teacher, nonetheless males receive more learning opportunities than females. Teachers pay more attention to males than females in their capacity as learners. It is probably safe to assume that some degree of gender stereotype is at work both in society at large and in schools and classrooms particularly. Boys are expected to achieve more in the long run than girls, therefore more teacher effort and attention is extended to them. Boys also are presumed to have more potential for acting out and general misbehavior than girls, even as early as the preschool years. Teachers tend to respond to these real and anticipated negative behaviors with more negative attention toward boys than girls.

The qualitative differences in teacher-initiated interactions also are important to examine. Teacher praise and criticism of boys tends to be different than it is for girls. Teachers are more likely to praise boys for their intellectual ability than girls, while girls receive more feedback and praise from teachers about the neatness and form of their work than boys. Criticism also may be differentiated by gender. Teachers more often criticize boys' work for lack of effort, while they more often criticize girls for their lack of academic or intellectual ability. Finally, the quality of questions asked of students also appears to differ by gender.

Teachers tend to ask more questions of male students that require higher levels of thinking than those asked of female students. The quality of academic feedback provided to males and the greater pressure exerted on males to find the answers and solve the problems place female students in a position where less achievement and a lower quality of achievement may be expected of them. The final result is that females may accomplish less than males due to the lower expectations of them—a situation of unequal educational outcomes.

In examining the entire picture of classroom interactions, one finds that, regardless of the age of the student, the gender of the teacher, or the content being taught, males are pressed to do more and to do it better by their teachers than are females. Girls are perceived to behave better, so they are less often the focus of discipline. Girls are more likely to go through the system with fewer challenges than boys; either to their behavior or their intellectual growth.

Some of the teachers discussed in this chapter tend to ignore the issue of gender stereotypes, which many believe society still sends in a powerful way. This point of view may be illustrated when the teacher considers each of the students strictly as an individual and goes from that point to help develop that student's potential in all aspects of classroom learning. Others of the teachers acknowledge the impact of stereotypical thinking that may have shaped the student's behavior and attitude toward achievement in school. These teachers tend to reach out to the students in groups of males and females and try to remediate these stereotypical messages. Further, the teacher may do this from a framework of thinking about gender issues in the context of either equality or equity. The former framework would require the teacher to carefully treat boys and girls absolutely equally, both in the quality and the quantity of interactions. The framework of equity would be illustrated through the interpretation of one group, by virtue of their gender, as being less empowered in general than the other. The most extreme example given is that of Beth, who works to empower the girls, sometimes to the near exclusion of the boys.

Judy consciously structures her interactions equally. While she is sensitive to the power of stereotypical messages her students receive in their daily lives, she insists on dealing with her students uniformly. Gender equity is rarely a topic taken up in a direct way. When students directly or indirectly exclude another child, Judy opens conversation with the children in the hope of creating cognitive conflict at a later date. She neither censures nor uses what she would refer to as propaganda. Children are not told to behave in a fair manner. They are prodded to analyze their own thinking of the situation and other situations that will follow. Judy's interactions with her students are very gender neutral—almost exactly the same for every child in a given situation, regardless of gender. Of the teachers discussed, Judy is most conscious of the issue of discipline as a critical gender consideration. She is aware that the boys in her class, during this academic year at least, tend to pull more of her attention toward them for punitive and disciplinary reasons. This is a point upon which she has reflected and chosen a particular action. She is careful not to be drawn into a pattern that has several components. She consciously interacts with the boys in a positive manner as often as possible, to offset the number of times her interactions might take on a negative quality. Further, she is conscious of the fact that a combination of disciplinary interactions and positive interactions would constitute far more interactions for the boys than the girls. Therefore, she is careful to give a piece of herself to each child as equally as possible.

Karen chooses to deal head-on with gender equity, as well as other societal issues. This is brought to bear through her interactions with the students. Karen is more likely than Judy to seek out students who need to experience non-traditional activities. Both quantitative as well as qualitative differences are apparent. Boys who tend not to participate in helping or nurturing situations and girls who shy away from block building activities tend to receive more of Karen's interactions than the other students, as she guides the stereotypically inclined students in directions they would not take on their own. Girls who show an interest in math or boys who sit quietly in the reading center may have slightly less and different attention than those pursuing their ordinary interests, if these interests represent gender stereotypes.

Students who are limiting themselves in their experiences or options may receive more direction and attention from Karen. This attention is personal, and tailored to their individual needs. In this way a qualitative difference is created. The other children certainly are paid attention to, but not quite as much and not with quite the same level of intensity.

Mary's interpretation of gender equity is explained as that of equality, as illustrated through her interactions with her students.

She makes her position about non-exclusionary practices clear to her students from the beginning of the school year. She also calls her students on overt sexist comments. With regard to her interactions, she is careful to allot the same quantity and quality to boys and girls. She exhibits a pattern of alternate questioning by gender, and asks both genders the same quality of questions. This is purposeful practice on her part. Her concerns about empowering girls in school are addressed through her interaction patterns, which provide girls with equal participation to that of boys, both quantitatively and qualitatively.

Sean focuses his implementation of gender equity through interaction patterns and classroom management. His monitoring of students could be described as a constant whirl of activity. Sean is always in motion, interacting with each student several times each class period as the students work on their projects. He works his way through the student tables in the same route each time, in order to ensure that all students receive the same amount of interaction time. The quality of his interactions also reflects his use of equal treatment for all students. His manner of individual instruction is that of questioning and prodding. Girls and boys are dealt with identically; they are urged to find their own solutions and press on in their work. Behavioral and academic expectations do not vary based on gender. Sean's teaching and interaction styles reflect his belief that all students can succeed in his class. Because he consciously works toward that end, regularly assessing his interaction patterns with his classes, he tends to meet this goal.

Beth's interaction pattern with her students demonstrates her commitment to enhancing the experiences of the girls in a content area traditionally considered to be masculine. On balance, she tends to draw the females into the class discussion more often than the males. This reflects her interpretation of gender equity as an issue where equitable rather than equal treatment is required. To offset the stereotypical notion that science is a place for male achievement, she insists that the girls in her class participate and succeed. The success of her approach is demonstrated through comments by the girls themselves, as well as very equal academic outcomes. Grades and achievement test scores do not show a pattern by gender.

Beth believes strongly that gender stereotypes dictate to a large degree how her students see themselves in relationship to their ability to succeed in school. She perceives this issue to be one that particularly affects females. Therefore, despite cultural and more general societal traditions that might be at odds with her feminist perspective, she presses her female students to take an active role in their schooling.

Whether the teacher committed to gender equity uses an equal or equitable framework is a matter of personal philosophy for these teachers. At issue here is not whether one approach is better than another, but rather which is the best fit for the individual teacher in his or her classroom practice. Each of these teachers is inspired by a need to create classroom dynamics that allow girls to have the opportunity to achieve as well as boys, and for boys not to face the bulk of discipline simply because of their gender, which may be influencing the teacher's preconceived notions that boys are more likely to misbehave than girls.

A second important point to consider about the illustrations of these teachers as they interact with their students within a context of gender equity is that each teacher acts based on thoughtful reflection of the power of their interaction patterns and style. Although different in many ways, each of the teachers consistently considers who she or he is questioning, how often, and at what level of complexity. None of their actions is accidental. All are aware that gender stereotyping continues, to varying degrees, to shape how students and teachers interact. These teachers acknowledge the long history of male domination, both positive and negative, in classrooms. They proceed to work toward ensuring that their interactions with their students, whether guided by an equal or equitable framework, further their goals for gender equity in their teaching.

CHAPTER 6

Toward Gender Equity in Your Classroom

The purpose of this final chapter is to provide an overview of issues involved in integrating gender equity into classroom practice, and to bring these issues further into the context of the classroom. The chapter is divided into several sections. We return first to a discussion of the frameworks of equal and equitable through a critical examination of the practices of Judy, Beth, and Karen. It will be helpful to keep the findings of the research in mind as you analyze the three teachers' approaches and continue to consider your own interpretation of gender equity.

The next section of the chapter is an examination of some of the challenges teachers face as they work toward gender equity in their classrooms. Discipline that is free of gender bias is one of these challenges, and may be one of the more difficult aspects of gender equity to achieve. The discipline practices of Judy, Mary, Sean, Fred, Bob, Karen, and Beth are addressed in order for the reader to gain insight into the various perspectives and dilemmas these teachers face as they consider this issue. As you read this part of the chapter, refer to the parts of chapter 5 regarding discipline and gender to gain a sense of the difficulty of connecting research findings that examine gender bias with real-life classroom practice that strives to foster gender equity. A second part of this section introduces the thoughts of the eight teachers as they reflect on various avenues of both support and resistance in their gender equity work. The comments of some of the teachers coincide with the issues addressed in chapter 2 regarding socialization and gender, and schools and gender.

The last section of this chapter, "Getting Started," discusses the importance of determining your own interpretation of gender equity as well as giving consideration to your position within the culture of your school. Finally, the teachers offer some advice to bring gender equity into your classroom practice.

EQUAL OR EQUITABLE?

While there is no quick fix for gender bias, there are several things to consider when setting out to incorporate gender equity into teaching. Perhaps the initial step is to reflect upon the conceptual frameworks that address the issue. The frameworks of equal and equitable both seek to remedy gender bias. However, the two represent different ways of interpreting gender equity.

This section revisits the classrooms of Judy, Beth, and Karen. Judy's classroom practices provide an opportunity to consider an interpretation of gender equity according to a framework of equality. Beth's classroom practice allows for an analysis of gender-equity teaching within an equitable framework. Karen's practice illustrates methods implemented within the framework of equality, while certain aspects of an equitable framework also are evident. As you begin to consider the two conceptual frameworks and how you might use the concepts offered by each, it is helpful to analyze their use in real classrooms.

Judy

Judy's goal for gender equity in her preschool classroom is firmly entrenched within the context of a framework of equality. There are other components of her philosophy that combine with the this framework to create a rather unique approach. Judy believes that all of her students should receive equal treatment. She provides learning experiences within the curriculum that incorporate both "masculine" and "feminine" activities. She also carefully selects her language and interactions so that her communication with the students is remarkably the same from one student to the next. Her language and actions are always void of gender representations or implicit gender bias. For example, she consciously does not praise male students for their physical prowess and female students for their prettiness or neatness, as the research indicates many other teachers do. Instead, students are addressed and interacted with regarding their business within the classroom and within the context of the learning activities for the day.

Judy's commitment to using cognitive conflict as a means to

allow students to develop the ability to question their assumptions and beliefs is actualized in the classroom in several ways. The most obvious technique she uses that reflects this method is interacting with children through probing and questioning. She does not tell a child that identifying pointed teeth as a male characteristic is silly. Instead, she questions the student about how he formed this belief and why. Judy is confident that, in the final analysis, this conversation will stay with the child and eventually remind him that if pointed teeth proved to be a misleading means of gender differentiation, there are probably other traits that he should disregard as gender specific.

Judy also consciously rejects the idea of purposefully mixing the students by gender. Doing so would be a violation of her belief that students must have the freedom to choose and make their own decisions about their work and their partners. She steadfastly rejects the idea that gender mixing engineered by her would have any value for the students in the long run. Ultimately, she believes the students will decide for themselves with whom they will interact and what values they will hold about issues such as gender equity.

Not surprisingly, the students' activities and the environment of the classroom as a whole reflect Judy's beliefs and actions regarding the integration of gender equity into her work. The three-, four-, and five-year-old children—girls, boys, special needs, and non-special needs alike—appear to take responsibility for themselves. Their ability to express themselves verbally grows during the school year, as does their ability to conduct themselves independently, with minimal adult guidance.

Also reflected in the classroom is distinct gender segregation. Girls and boys do not interact with each other, nor do boys and girls often enter the other gender's play "domain." Given the free choice of cooking or anything else, the boys choose other than cooking. Similarly, the blocks are seldom visited by the girls. The invitation from Judy to the students to participate in activities other than those traditionally associated with their gender is usually not accepted by the students. The result is that by the end of the school year, many of the students have not experienced all of the activities across the curriculum. Instead they tend to stick with those activities traditionally linked with their own gender.

Judy's interpretation of gender equity is a very clear example of Secada's (1989) description of the equality framework. It focuses on a concern of "inputs." The teacher cares a great deal that the students receive the most equal opportunity and access to learning as possible. The "outcomes" are a less immediate concern. While Judy does care how her students consider issues of gender as they grow older, her gender equity teaching is focused on the daily world of her classroom. The fact that her students are not integrated by gender in her classroom does not concern her so much. She believes that her cognitive-conflict approach is a more powerful means of changing attitudes in the long run than is overt engineering of students' beliefs.

In a sense, Judy operates on blind faith regarding the power and success of her cognitive-conflict method because there is not a simple means of assessing the success of her techniques. The conversations she has with the various children about their assumptions and beliefs that occur when an incident arises often end without closure. The child is left to consider the implications of the discussion on her or his own. Judy probably will never know whether the child got the point, and if so, how the child's understanding of the issue affected her or his attitudes and behavior later on.

The issue of open-endedness and ambiguity about the extent of Judy's success regarding gender equity would be problematic for many teachers. Most of us need more immediate feedback about whether or not our methods work. However, for those who believe strongly in the efficacy of the individual's right to make decisions and develop values free of adult coercion and manipulation, Judy's means of implementing gender equity through a framework of equality, shaped by her interpretation of cognitive conflict, may be the only approach that is right for her.

Beth

Beth's goal for gender equity extends further than the confines of her classroom. Inherent in her adoption of an equitable framework for her work with gender issues is the belief that outcomes are the essential consideration. To attempt to give all of her students equal opportunity and access would not address the more far-reaching goal of equal outcomes between the gender groups. She has determined that more aggressive measures must be taken in order for the girls in her classroom as well as other girls in the school to attain the same skills and knowledge in science, as well as of themselves, as the boys.

Within the classroom walls, she attempts to enhance the participation and success of the girls, even to the occasional exclusion of boys' participation. She believes her approach is justified through a liberal interpretation of gender bias. That is, she believes that as a group, females are less empowered within the general society and receive fewer opportunities and options within schools than males. This is an especially pressing point for Beth inasmuch as she teaches science, long considered a masculine domain. In order to counter the effects of this perceived systematic gender bias, she focuses more of her resources on the girls than the boys. In this way, she hopes to compensate for what has happened to the girls in other classes and for what they may encounter in the future. If they are armed with self-assurances that they can succeed in her science classroom, Beth expects the girls will be more likely to succeed in future science classes as well as in other aspects of their lives.

Within the community of the school, Beth attempts to incorporate as many of the girls as possible. She believes that schools are structurally gender biased; male achievement, both athletic and scholastic, tends to be accorded higher value than female achievement. To counter the effects of the systematic bias she perceives, she delivers more resources to the girls than the boys with special events. The girls-only field trips, visits by women's athletic teams, and mother-daughter forums are examples.

Beth's general perceptions of gender bias in schools are supported by the research. Males do tend to dominate classrooms and in general benefit more from the academic and athletic opportunities provided by schools. However, as we consider the appropriateness of gender equity according to an equitable framework, an important point should be considered. At the heart of this interpretation is the belief in systematic bias and inequity. While it is hard to argue that gender bias exists, the question is whether or not the teacher, in this case Beth, has accurately assessed the extent of the bias. Has she correctly determined the degree to which all female students have experienced exclusion or inequitable opportunity? Beth's assessment of societal bias is the only means upon which she can judge the appropriateness of her gender equity measures. Her interpretation of the extent to which gender bias exists in society dictates how she will address gender equity in her teaching. Of course, Beth's interpretation is not necessarily the same as others' interpretations. To that end, her practices might be judged to be too extreme by some, and not extreme enough by others. In the final analysis, various interpretations of the issues surrounding gender bias can create very different methods and degrees of solutions for the problem. Gender equity according to an equitable framework is solely based on the individual's own assessment of the magnitude of the problem and the measures necessary to address it.

In his effort to more clearly define the framework of equity as opposed to equality, Secada (1989) discusses another problem inherent in attempting to work within an equitable framework. He contends that from the outset we create the problem of categorizing people into groups, which in turn may obscure their needs as individuals:

> When we create groups and assign individuals to them, regardless how well-intentioned that grouping is, we also have taken steps to marginalize and to dehumanize the members of the other group, the one to which we do not belong. The danger in assigning individuals to groups is that "we homogenize outsiders; we impose an objective interpretation of group membership in full confidence . . . that our beliefs are well founded, that our ways of sorting people out are good and right" (Green 1987, 6 in Secada 1989, 83).

An interpretation of gender equity illustrated through Beth's classroom practice relies on the assumption that, as a member of the female group, each girl requires more resources delivered to her than any boy requires. The nature of the framework suggests that individual students' needs are less focused upon than the perceived needs of the group. Certainly it is bound to be the case that in any science classroom some of the male students will require extra attention in order to succeed. Similarly, a reading class will have girls who require additional resources from the teacher in order to succeed. Do these students, members of the group perceived to need less, become casualties of gender bias themselves?

As with many of the dilemmas surrounding our attempts to be more egalitarian in our society, there is no definitive solution to the problems of gender bias and no absolute prescription for addressing gender equity in classroom teaching. However, there may be some logic in borrowing from both the equal and the equitable interpretations when developing a personal approach. Of the eight teachers profiled in the book, Karen's understanding and everyday integration of gender equity into her teaching illustrates a combination of the two frameworks. To this point, Karen's classroom practice has been shown principally as an example of an equality interpretation of gender equity. Without question, her daily teaching portrays focus on inputs. However, the foundation of her philosophy regarding gender issues tends to be imbedded in an equitable framework.

Karen

Karen's interpretation of gender equity has been analyzed primarily as one of equality with a general focus on inputs. Karen is concerned that all of her students receive the same opportunities and access to learning, despite gender. However, as has been illustrated throughout the chapters, Karen is unwilling to allow her students to choose gender segregation.

From the beginning of the school year, Karen both overtly and more subtly creates an environment that promotes gender equity. She and the students discuss the meaning of the words and concepts having to do with gender bias. She directly teaches the students her views of the inadequacies of interpreting life through rigid gender roles. Before long, the students can articulate some of the more concrete issues of gender bias; for example, that males and females can do the same things.

In addition to her direct teaching about what she refers to as "gender equitable living," Karen also engineers gender-mixed learning and socializing situations. Her student committees are established such that girls and boys are responsible for working together. In addition, she does not allow the students continually to choose some activities to the exclusion of others.

While some choice does lie with the individual student, Karen monitors who is in which center from one day to the next. Girls who appear to be avoiding the block area, for example, are maneuvered in that direction. Similarly, boys avoiding the reading/listening center are compelled to spend some time there. All students experience all aspects of the curriculum, whether that is their preference or not.

There is visible evidence on a daily basis of the success of Karen's approach to gender equity in her classroom. Her students are sensitive to gender bias in language, and periodically talk about it. On at least a superficial level, they know that females and males are equal in abilities and should be equal in opportunities. "Boys and girls can both do that" is a common statement by the children when literature, careers, or other topics are discussed. However, the most striking evidence of the success of Karen's gender integration is the unconscious gender mixing that takes place within the work groups and at the door when lining up. Boys and girls work collaboratively and offer help to one another with cleaning chores. At the door they automatically pair up with whomever is handy. On every occasion, most of the pairs, usually holding hands, are girl-boy, and of different cultural backgrounds, as well. Karen's class reflects gender integration that is both consciously and unconsciously played out by the students. Karen's concentration on inputs and her aggressive work to ensure that gender segregation does not exist in the class result in daily outcomes that show her that what she is doing works. Spontaneously mixed gender cooperation and play are good examples of this.

Karen believes that she is laying a foundation of experience for her students in their understanding of gender bias and gender equity. She hopes the learning in the kindergarten room will provide a foundation of beliefs and skills that students will take with them through their schooling. Whether this happens and the extent to which her students eventually live in an equitable manner is more difficult to assess. Karen integrates gender equity into her teaching with the hope that the foundation she supplies for her students will establish within them a permanent value system that will contain affirmation of gender equity.

Certain aspects of Karen's practice also reflect an equitable framework. Karen believes that issues of gender and bias are pivotal concerns for the larger society, as well as for the microcosm of that society which is her classroom. Consistent within this framework, she believes that society is constructed in a gender biased fashion, with accompanying and powerful gender role stereotypes that dictate and reinforce the existence of gender bias. Although the girls as a group may be socialized such that they tend to exhibit more school-readiness traits as they enter kindergarten, she believes it is the boys as a group who eventually will be more empowered by the structure of the school and society as a whole. Females are more at-risk for not successfully competing in our dominant culture than are males.

Karen initially identifies her students as members of one gender group or the other. She thinks of her girls and her boys as being likely to exhibit different sets of interests and behaviors that have been shaped by gender stereotypes. To that end, she uses gender as a characteristic to guide her monitoring of her students' participation in classroom activities. She watches carefully for girls who seem to be confining themselves to a limited set of interests and activities that can be construed as stereotypically feminine. Similarly, she is alert to her male group of students, among whom may be boys who tend to exhibit only instrumental characteristics and accompanying behaviors. Her belief in a gender-biased societal structure leads her to be wary of stereotypic patterns into which her students may fall.

At the same time, on a daily basis, Karen clearly attempts to distribute the learning resources in her classroom in an equal fashion. All children receive the same quantity and quality of interaction and access to all aspects of the curriculum, and are exposed to non-sexist and anti-sexist language and classroom organization. However, in addition to considering the students as members of one gender group or the other, Karen evaluates the unique needs of each student. The result is that each child receives equal learning opportunity and access, but this is accorded based on the individual child's need. While Karen is sensitive to issues of prevailing gender stereotypes and the impact of them on the students in her class, she also is sensitive to the idea that some children exhibit characteristics, interests, and strengths in school that are not based on gender stereotypes. In other words, while she believes that patterns of stereotyping influence do exist, so do the exceptions to these patterns. She acknowledges that boys may be more likely than girls to settle disputes physically, act aggressively, and work independently, but she knows she always will have boys who are quiet, sensitive, and greatly in need of nurturance.

Karen provides an example of a teacher committed to gender equity who is conscious of the concepts of both equity and equality. Her words, which reflect her interpretation of gender equity, and the way her classroom operates demonstrate this. Karen acknowledges that the power of gender stereotypes cannot be ignored, that these stereotypes often play a large role in how students think and act, and in how dynamics are played out in classrooms. However, her understanding of the uniqueness of the individual compels Karen to disregard the student's gender when it becomes clear that the student does not require measures that would help her or him overcome the barriers of stereotypic attitudes.

This illustration of the interpretation and implementation of gender equity by Judy, Beth, and Karen helps explain how some teachers go about integrating gender equity into their teaching according to equal and equitable frameworks, and a combination of equal and equitable frameworks, respectively. Some teachers are most comfortable in attempting to provide each of their students as equal an amount of resources as possible. Others feel strongly that to implement gender equity through this framework simply is not enough; that extending extra and uneven resources to female learners is the only means of addressing the goal of gender equity. Female students as a group cannot hope to reap the benefits of schooling similarly to male students without receiving some additional measure of support from the teacher. Finally, some may find that Karen provides an appropriate model. The foundation of her work in gender equity is built on an understanding of the issue as equitable, and to some extent she constructs her classroom accordingly. Her assumptions about pervasive gender bias in society guide her methods of direct and insistent intervention in her attempts to modify her students' value systems and/or behavioral patterns that reflect their learned stereotypic behavior.

All of the three teachers work hard to realize their articulated goals for gender equity in their classrooms. There are distinct differences among them, and as you continue to consider the place of gender equity in your teaching, you must determine which is the best approach for you.

CHALLENGES FOR INTEGRATING GENDER EQUITY

To varying degrees, the eight teachers profiled work to integrate gender equity into their teaching. There are some problems along the way, however. In the following section two challenges these teachers encountered are examined. Disciplining students in ways that do not reflect gender bias can be a challenge even to teachers who give substantial consideration to this issue. Of all of the aspects of gender-sensitive teaching examined, bias-free discipline proved to be a particularly difficult area for some of the teachers to successfully implement.

A second point considered in this section is the teachers' perception of support for or resistance to their efforts. Teaching in general can be an occupation that is done in isolation. However, when teachers attempt to construct classrooms which may be at odds with the general culture of the surrounding community or that of the school, they may encounter resistance from the administration or their colleagues that may add to a sense of isolation.

Discipline

To this point the gender-equity teaching practices of the eight teachers profiled have, for the most part, illustrated thoughtful reflection and implementation of positive methods as the teachers attempt to counter gender bias in their classrooms. One important aspect of good gender-equity teaching practice that did not fare as well as most other aspects was that of unbiased discipline practices. As you consider the profiled teachers as models for good gender-equity teaching, it is well to keep in mind that none of the classrooms exemplified the perfect scenario of gender equity in teaching, especially when compared to the results and suggestions of the research. More than any other issue, discipline carried out by some of the teachers proved to be affected by gender bias.

The research suggests that discipline is an aspect of classroom life that tends to be affected strongly by gender bias. It also is one of the few aspects of gender equity in which a case can be made that male students often feel the effects of gender bias more than female students.

A number of the teachers studied discussed the issue of gender-differentiated discipline in their classrooms. They believe that in their classrooms they regularly encounter misbehavior that they consider to be gender related. Some teachers reported that they work to overcome their tendency to discipline the boys for "typical boy" behavior to the exclusion of disciplining the girls for their misbehavior. Several of the teachers remarked that they did not differentiate by gender in disciplining their students at all. Yet the observations indicated a strong pattern of boys receiving the lion's share of verbal warnings as well as removals from the classroom, despite these teachers' perceptions of their actions regarding discipline and gender.

The discipline practices of Mary, Sean, and Fred are discussed next. Each of these teachers demonstrates patterns of gender bias in their discipline practices. Mary does so quite unconsciously and in a way that conflicts with her commitment to and understanding of gender equity. Sean and Fred are aware of their tendencies to discipline boys more often than girls. Each gives insight into their thinking about their discipline patterns.

Mary believes she regularly encounters gender-differentiated behavior among her students. In describing her students within the context of leadership ability, Mary sees a pattern of behavior by gender that reflects many of the larger societal messages about gender roles.

> The boys are more likely to be playground leaders. The girls are more likely to extend that to the classroom as well as out to the playground. At this age, I think the girls are more powerful in terms of how they choose to utilize that, and I think they use it in more harmful ways. This is only my third year, but I've seen the same thing each year. The girls are more apt to be exclusionary, on the basis of looks, academic success, or whether or not you take gymnastics, or if you just know the right people or go to the right places. The boys at this age who are apt to be exclusionary, it's really more on the soccer field. And it tends to revolve around the game, rather than around the person. With girls, I get feedback about hurt. It's personal: "So and so wouldn't play with me," or "So and so said something about me."

Mary is conscious of these gender-differentiated behaviors that permeate her classroom. She is aware that the boys and girls may act according to stereotypic expectations that are well entrenched; in this case, boys are invested in winning the game, while the girls are concerned with relationships among those playing the game. Despite Mary's sensitivity to some behavior patterns by gender, there remains a strong pattern of boys being on the receiving end of most of the discipline. The hours of observation revealed that no girls were disciplined, while five boys were repeatedly disciplined. These boys' seats were moved, they were verbally reprimanded, and one was removed from the class. Several times girls were observed doing many of the same things the boys were disciplined for: talking and being out of their seats wandering around the room. The girls were ignored or simply not noticed, while the boys were redirected. The girls and boys in Mary's class who misbehaved appeared to do the same things; however, it was the boys who received the discipline. Despite Mary's commitment to do otherwise, her pattern of disciplining the third graders reflected gender bias.

The same pattern evolved in Sean's classroom. In Sean's discussion of gender-related behaviors within the context of teacher-initiated interactions, it was evident that he has considered this issue. Further, he is not reticent about describing boys as the group who are his primary behavior problems. He believes that gender-related behaviors are due largely to societal gender-role messages accepted by many boys; to be masculine is to test the limits, often in verbally and physically aggressive ways. He believes this accounts for his own pattern of disciplining boys far more often than girls.

The hours of observation in Sean's classes did reveal a strong pattern of male students being on the receiving end of verbal reprimands, redirection, and threats of being sent to the office. Only one girl was spoken to once about her inability to settle down to the task at hand, even though there were numerous times when she and other girls in the two classes were as off-task as the boys to whom Sean spoke.

Fred, too, acknowledges differences in discipline by gender. His discussion of the issue tends to be directed more to his own actions rather than to the behaviors of the students.

> I think I may be more used to males. I had all brothers. While the behavior problems I have are pretty much the same for girls and boys—tardies and talking—I have a tendency, if it's a girl, to talk to them more. If it's a guy, I feel I can be harsher or more blunt. Sometimes I feel that the girls are more of a problem because I don't get right to the point.

Fred believes that he treats the students differently by gender when discipline is involved. Indeed, observation data substantiate his assessment of the problem.

Talking and tardiness were the extent of Fred's discipline concerns during the observations. In equal numbers, girls and boys arrived late or chatted with their neighbors during independent work. Fred's response to the girls' talking was to walk over to them and have a whispered, private conversation. His disciplinary techniques for the boys who were engaged in the same behaviors were different. Boys were addressed publicly from the front of the room by Fred. The boys' seats were moved to the outskirts of the seating arrangement, or in several cases, the boys were removed from the room altogether.

Fred has correctly assessed his behavior as gender differentiated. He also is aware that he is disciplining his students in a gender biased fashion. His next step is to begin to rectify the problem.

Discipline in the classrooms of Judy, Bob, Karen, and Beth is discussed next. The discipline practiced by each of these teachers provides contrast to the previous three examined. Although there is more variation than similarity among these teachers, they have all developed means of addressing discipline in ways that reflect gender equity.

A useful way to analyze the gender-equitable discipline practices of these teachers is to draw once again on the frameworks of equality and equity. Discipline that reflects gender equity and is done according to the framework of equality might be thought of as that which focuses on process, or inputs. Put in operational terms, the teacher would apply rules and consequences consistently to both girls and boys. If fighting occurs or inappropriate language is used, students receive identical punishment regardless of gender. Further, if boys fight or use inappropriate language more often than girls, boys are disciplined more often than girls.

Discipline constructed through the an equitable framework focuses on outcomes. According to this approach, a teacher applying discipline equitably would worry about administering the same amount of attention across genders, so that in the final analysis neither boys nor girls as a group would receive more negative attention than the other. This means of interpreting discipline might compel the teacher to ignore some behaviors in one gender group of students while he or she would respond to the same behaviors in the other group. For example, if fighting or inappropriate language is more often a problem with the boys in the class, the teacher might consciously choose to ignore some of this behavior on the part of the boys so that, in the end, the amount of disciplinary attention given to the boys does not overshadow that given to the girls. As in the case of other issues within gender equity, discipline that is either free from gender bias or reflective of it can be analyzed within the frameworks of equality or equity.

As you may recall from the earlier discussion in chapter 5, Judy is quite conscious of gender-differentiated behaviors on the part of her preschoolers. She believes that the boys will be more likely to be boisterous and less likely than girls to sit attentively. Boys are more likely to break the classroom rules that have to do with physical aggression and working quietly to allow others to do their work. As a result of her reflection about this, she attempts to interact with the boys on a positive note in equal measure with the girls.

The observations revealed that during Judy's monitoring of the centers, it was the handful of loud boys who commanded nearly all of her discipline-related attention. She quieted them down and on occasion redirected their play, as in the case of the assaults on the dolls in the home center. As she discussed, she did work to give the boys positive attention as well. But without question, boys were the recipients of discipline far more often than girls.

As in all other aspects of her gender-equitable teaching practice, Judy constructs discipline within the framework of equality. Judy is concerned with discipline as a process issue; students who break classroom rules are spoken to in the same fashion and receive the same consequences regardless of their gender. In Judy's classroom this particular year, several of the boys are aggressive and loud. They are the ones who receive the redirection. Given a different classroom composition, one or more girls might demonstrate the same behaviors as the boys this year, and receive the identical consequences. In Judy's classroom, despite the child's gender, breaking a specific rule holds a specific consequence.

Bob also spoke of gender specific behaviors of his students with regard to discipline. While he believes he has few discipline problems, he is very aware of the discipline incidents representing patterns of behavior that tend to be gender specific.

> There do seem to be different types of discipline problems. Certainly, the boy you observed who was being really obnoxious verbally represents what would tend to be a more typical male response of being assertive and obnoxious. I think that is a result of a more traditional upbringing on the part of that student. He has been trained to be assertive and obnoxious. I find that many of the girls also show what I would consider traditional "girl" behavioral problems; namely being bitchy. Yes, the behavioral problems do seem to be according to traditional gender patterns.

Bob's assessment of having few behavioral problems in his class was borne out in the observation data. The casual classroom climate he has created, combined with an expectation that the students should be self starters and monitor themselves, result in Bob seldom raising his voice above the considerable din. The only interactions he had with students that remotely could be considered of a disciplinary nature were on several occasions when he spoke about students getting back to work. During these times he tended to address groups at a table, rather than individually. The reminders were gentle, and usually took the form of: "I see that we're already several minutes into the class and table 7 doesn't seem to be working. I would suggest the people at that table get going."

Ignoring most of the minor misbehaviors is Bob's usual response to discipline. He does this for "girl" and "boy" behaviors. When redirection is necessary, Bob's usual method is to speak to a group as a whole. For example, table 7 is gender mixed, as are most of the tables. Because he tends not to redirect students individually, the boys and girls get the same message at the same time. When a more major offense has been committed and redirection of an individual student is required, he responds to girls in the same way as he does to boys. To that end, he demonstrates no gender bias in his dealings with students through discipline. His approach is consistent with his interpretation of gender equity as an issue of equality. He ignores both "boy obnoxiousness" and "girl bitchiness" whether these behaviors are demonstrated by a boy or a girl. He also enforces consequences for more serious violations regardless of gender.

Karen also appears to have escaped gender-biased discipline practices. Her acknowledgement of the presence of gender role stereotypes combined with her careful assessment of the needs of each student as an individual create a discipline scenario without a gender-related pattern. Instead, "boy" misbehaviors, whether committed by a boy or girl, are dealt with based on the misbehavior rather than on the gender of who committed it. Consistent with her implementation of many other methods, Karen disciplines her students within a framework of equality. Her emphasis is on process. She applies a standard of discipline regardless of the gender of the child misbehaving. Bob's and Karen's approaches are different, fitting their personal teaching styles, are consistent with their interpretation of gender equity issues, and are the products of reflection.

Beth's interpretation of discipline is through an equitable lens, as are all other aspects of gender equity in her teaching. Because this is her approach, she is concerned about the outcome of her discipline process, not only as it affects the students' behavior but also as it affects the gender groups in her classes.

Beth applies a form of behavioristic discipline. At the beginning of the school year, Beth explains the classroom rules as well as the consequences of breaking the rules. From that point on, she enforces her policies without explanation. A first-time rule breaker receives his or her name on the board. A check mark is placed next to the student's name when the student breaks a rule a second time, with more checks appearing next to the student's name if she or he misbehaves repeatedly. The students know, for example, that two checks mean a short detention after school. Four checks indicate a call home and a parent conference. Beth's discipline method is similar to those used in many other classrooms. What makes Beth's method slightly different from others is that she carefully monitors her use of checks during each period in order to be sure that neither boys nor girls as a group are receiving more checks than the other.

> I don't think boys get their names on the board more often than girls. By this age, girls have more complete discipline than boys, so they can control themselves better if they don't want to get another check. Girls tend to get checks for talking or writing notes. Boys usually get checks for more aggressive behavior. But I always watch to be sure that there are the same number of checks for boys and girls.

Because Beth focuses on the outcome, or a balance of checks by gender, she sometimes finds herself ignoring behaviors that she considers fairly minor, by girls at times and boys at other times. She does this as she weighs the distribution of check marks by gender groups so there is no bias according to the amount of discipline across genders. Her discipline strongly reflects her interpretation of this issue as an equitable one.

The issue of discipline as an aspect of gender bias is an interesting one. It is apparent from the illustrations of the classrooms of some of the teachers profiled that, despite their commitment to gender equity, some often discipline in a biased fashion. These findings are consistent with those reported in the research literature. Disciplining in a way that reflects gender equity is more difficult than it would first appear. Young boys who display traditional masculine traits may have difficulty meeting expectations of "good" school behavior. For example, staying on task, remaining quiet, and staying in one's seat are behaviors that are praised and reinforced in schools. These behaviors are traditionally reinforced in girls and not boys. Therefore, it is not surprising to find girls more often "well behaved" while boys as a group display behaviors that are inappropriate in the classroom more often. As a result, boys may get disciplined more often than girls, and for offenses that may be ignored in girls.

As it has been pointed out, even teachers like Mary, who are very aware of the issue may unconsciously do exactly the opposite of what they intend: practice in gender-biased ways through their patterns of disciplining students. Judy, Bob, Karen, and Beth may have escaped this problem, for several reasons. All are very conscious of the issue, and Judy, Bob, and Karen monitor themselves as they teach to be sure they are dealing with the discipline, rather than the student based on her or his gender. Their classrooms are different, but the means of discipline, which is framed in equality, is similar. Judy moves among her students constantly, Karen has her students move to her, while Bob tends to remain at his desk in front of the room. However, all three are aware of the behavior of their students at all times, and when the need arises they remind a misbehaving student of the rule and then redirect him or her. On other occasions, Judy, Bob, and Karen may observe a breach of the rules but choose to ignore it. Again, their choice to ignore is based on the degree of seriousness of the rule that has been broken rather than whether a girl or boy committed the offense. Beth also is very aware of her discipline practices. But instead of concentrating on the way standards of discipline are applied, she focuses on the balance of disciplinary attention across genders.

While many teachers may come to the conclusion that boys do indeed tend to need discipline in ways that girls as a group do not, it is important for teachers to carefully monitor their pattern of discipline and the form it takes. While many teachers make the case that boys, traditionally molded to be more aggressive and acting out, create more problems than girls, it is well to remember that reaching this sort of conclusion can result in discipline patterns where the teacher ignores "boy" misbehaviors in girls, but catches them in boys.

Support and Resistance

Effective classroom teaching that is enhanced through gender equity teaching practice is not commonly found in schools. The work of the teachers profiled in this book represent a minority perspective. These teachers are involved in work that is not likely part of the tradition or culture of the school. Perhaps for this reason they are very conscious of the level of support or resistance they receive in their endeavors.

Regardless of the framework and means adopted by the teachers in their integration of gender equity into their teaching, most of the teachers cited frustrations and barriers that they felt hampered their efforts. Some felt their students' parents needed to possess a greater understanding of the issues surrounding gender equity in order to help them work more effectively with the students in overcoming limiting stereotypic attitudes on the part of the students. Others described colleagues who were insensitive at best and overtly sexist at worst. One teacher talked about her principal, who she felt was unwilling to consider the gender bias within the structure of the school. Several of the teachers clearly felt appreciated and supported in their pursuit of gender equity. Support from administrators and colleagues was cited. The insights of the teachers into this aspect of teaching toward gender equity are useful as you contemplate your current or future teaching situation.

Judy's situation is unique among the others profiled, in that she has considerable control over who become her colleagues. She established the preschool program, and as director is responsible for hiring the teachers and aides. Because Judy sees gender equity, as well as other issues of equity, as critical considerations for the preschool program, she tends to select staff who share a concern about gender equity.

> As a staff, it's a shared value. Last year that wasn't so. I had two very young teachers. They didn't know what this had to do with anything. They saw the rest of us as bleeding-heart liberals. Maybe to some extent it's an age and generational issue. One of the things I didn't want to do when I started to put staff together was hire everybody like me. Now that's what I'm doing. It just has to do with gathering like-minded people.

The obvious benefit of having all staff at the preschool regard the issue of gender equity as a shared value is that there is substantial consistency as the various aspects of gender equity are integrated into the program. Judy can exert control over this, and it is easier for her vision and interpretation of gender equity to be integrated throughout the program.

However, Judy does not function with absolute autonomy. There are many people who have input into the preschool program: Judy's supervisor, the school district superintendent, the director of special education, the school board, and of course the parents of the students. Judy described some of the difficulties she feels hamper her efforts:

> I think some people are more aware than others. For example, the person who was my immediate supervisor last year had no clue about issues of gender equity. She won a beauty contest in 1982. She conducts herself as a beauty queen. The world has always worked for her when she does that. She can't see that there might be bigger issues.
>
> There are other, more subtle forms of resistance. Sometimes I get word that there is concern about the attire worn by staff. It's couched in professional ways; that the women should come to work in more feminine dress. I hear concerns about the weight of some of the staff. Weight is one issue that's very mixed in with sexism; the thinner the woman, the better she is, even in the workplace.

Judy cites some of the larger societal issues regarding gender bias that intrude into the work of the staff at the preschool. She firmly believes that teachers there need to come to work prepared to get dirty with the children as they play and that the traditional view of the ideal woman—thin and pretty—has no business in the workplace, or anywhere else for that matter.

There also are frustrations she describes with regard to attitudes of some parents:

> Some parents have a definite commitment. Some come in and say to me "I want to know what your school philosophy is in regard to gender issues." My guess to why that is, is because we have professional parents. They're educated and think things through.
>
> When talking to some parents, the statements we make are subtle. We tell them we have certain expectations about how children should come dressed to school, and that's dressed to play. Party clothes are not appropriate. That has to do most often with girls. We won't allow aggressive toys in school. That's a gender issue that's most often related to boys. When we have parents come in to talk about their professions, we try to get non-traditional people, and that is a message to parents. Then there are even more subtle things, such as when children

come in the door. We don't comment on what they're wearing. Although some parents try to pull us back into that form of gender bias (the parents of girls are the ones who are the most dependent on comments about how nice their daughters look). They say, "Oh, look at what she's wearing." I don't think we are militant in our values. We have statements in our parent handbooks about accepted differences. We do not say this is how it's going to be, and if you're doing it differently, you're doing it wrong. We just try to be an example.

As in her interactions with the children, Judy does not directly attempt to address gender bias she sees in the attitudes and behaviors of the parents. Instead, she suggests options for them to follow. For example, upon admission to the school, she mentions to the parents that children get dirty when playing, and that dressy and expensive clothes may get ruined. Regardless, several of the girls always are dressed in designer outfits. Julie sees this as the parents' choice, and she does not take the point up with them again. However, she refuses to reinforce the girls for their appearance, which easily could have the consequence of the girls trying to stay neat and clean, while the boys get down to the business of active play.

Not surprisingly, the bulk of Judy's support for her work in gender equity in the preschool comes from her colleagues. As the staff members join the school, Judy can be sure that they share a commitment to gender equity. The resistance Judy encounters tends to be in the context of broad gender-bias issues. The suggestions that the teachers and aides ought to dress more "professionally" (skirts, stockings, and high-heeled shoes), as well as the tendency of some parents to expect reinforcement of gender-specific and stereotypic traits in their children by school staff (party shoes and ruffled dresses for the girls; guns and war toys for the boys), are issues that she can deal with during the teaching day with the children.

In a very real sense, Karen's efforts regarding gender equity as well as other aspects of integration are supported through the structure of the school in which she teaches. The primary magnet school was conceived of from the beginning as being a catalyst for change in attitudes about race, ethnic, and class differences. In much the same way as Judy's staff hold shared commitments, so do the teachers, aides, and principal at Karen's school. Karen and her colleagues work toward helping each child develop self-

respect and respect for others, both through the celebration of differences and the development of a strong sense of community.

A conscious and concentrated effort toward gender equity is
not necessarily something all staff work toward to the same
extent, however. Karen stated:

> Sometimes I mention things about phraseology. I might call
> attention to a teacher's use of the phrase "You guys." I think
> kids see that as referring to males. Or I might bring up the point
> that words in a song should be changed because there are too
> many "hes." Some people look at me as if I'm from a different
> planet.

Karen said she would like to see the staff's commitment to the
reduction of bias include more attention to issues of gender. But in
the end, she is philosophical about it.

> It's sort of like losing weight. Nobody can do it for you. You
> have to get there by yourself. If that's not an area you're pas-
> sionate about, it's probably not an area you're going to make
> great leaps in. And it's not a passion for everyone.

Consistent with her perspective of gender equity through the
equitable framework, Beth speaks of forms of resistance that have
to do not only with daily encounters in the classroom, but also
with the broader scope of the school. In general, she feels good
about the impact of her gender equity work on her students.
Within the confines of the classroom, she is fairly autonomous
and has control over much of what she teaches and how she
teaches. Having an impact within the broader context of the
school proves more difficult. Beth's principal and many of her colleagues are far less interested in and committed to issues of gender.
As a result, Beth is frustrated by her failure to successfully tackle
the systematic gender bias she perceives to exist in her school.

Beth feels that the school principal, who was a feminist
activist herself twenty years ago, is sympathetic to some of the
issues, but does not extend herself far enough to correct many of
the inequities Beth perceives exist within the school.

> In all honesty, I would have to say I get some resistance from the
> principal. She has me shut up about some things. There was a
> situation when a male teacher showed a movie to his class with
> Audrey Hepburn in it. During the movie, he was panting and
> making lewd remarks about her. The kids told me about this. So

when we got together for organizing things for Women's Month, I told the principal about it. I said, "You know, this is going on." Another teacher said, "We ought to publish a newsletter with inappropriate things that people say or do that are sexist, but make it funny. I said, "Great, let's start with that one." The principal said, "No, I don't want it to get home to the parents."

There's another teacher who calls boys who can't hit a baseball well "faggots" and "wimps." Or he says, "You can go play with the girls if you can't do any better than that." So that does go on, and it gets kind of discouraging. I'm concerned on the kids' part. It's not right not to do something about this sort of thing.

Another thing that I think is a women's issue here at school is this: The men here just get away with a lot. They don't show up in classes. For example, we have two men that, if you went to their classes right now, they wouldn't be there yet. One morning I called the principal and told her I thought it was disgusting, but nothing happened. The two men have drinking problems, and they were probably drinking again, and when they got to class they were probably yelling at the kids the way they do when they're like that.

Beth sees another aspect of resistance in the form of lack of interest or sensitivity.

Most of the women faculty members are very supportive. In general, they really love any activities that end up happening that relate to the girls and women in the school. But at the same time, a lot of them think I'm too much. A woman at our school was collecting supermarket receipts so our school could buy computers. She was going to come into the room and tell the kids, "When your mom does the shopping, she should save the receipts." I told her it would be great if she would include the dads in the shopping spree. I could tell her reaction was, "Oh, can it. It's not that important." I get that from some people. But most of the women here see it once it's pointed out.

Despite her irritation with the principal for what she perceives as relative lack of support for gender issues related to the context of the school, and her frustration with teachers who either cannot or will not see the importance of the issues, Beth continues to press her points. Her support from a number of colleagues (all women) and her commitment to the girls in the school prompt her to carry on her efforts in gender equity.

In speaking about his perceptions of support regarding his work with gender equity, Bob described a scenario fairly common to many teachers, that of isolation. As many high-school teachers do, Bob has a fair amount of autonomy in the content and methods he adopts for his teaching. He integrates gender equity into his teaching because he feels it is an important issue in the lives of his students. However, gender equity is not an issue that receives attention school-wide. In fact, Bob sees his colleagues acting individually and collectively in gender stereotypic ways. He believes they are antithetical models for a healthy school climate regarding gender issues.

> My colleagues, in general being older and not having had the exposure to new educational programs, or avoiding them, are not aware that they are exhibiting biases. There are several members of the staff who are very biased. They really are—in a joking way, but nevertheless they are. In fact, there are things that happen that show lots of sexism and are accepted by the faculty. We had a faculty basketball game. What happened was the men played the game and the women acted as cheerleaders. The school where I taught before, the faculty basketball game had mixed-gender teams. But here, I don't think anyone thought anything about it.

Bob is unhappy that these messages are received by the students. He feels that he works with faculty who not only ignores gender issues in their work in their classrooms, but also produces modeling for the students that reinforces gender stereotypes.

On the positive side, Bob sees the gender makeup of the school administration as providing good modeling for the girls and boys, as well as the teachers, in the school.

> I think having a woman principal helps a lot. We also have a competent assistant principal who is a woman. These are women in authority positions who are accorded respect. This sends a subconscious message, but I think it has greater impact than all the verbal tricks you could pull.

The issues Bob cites are common in high schools. Teachers often work in isolation, concentrating on relaying the content to their students. When collaboration occurs, it tends to be directed to issues of which content to include in the curriculum. Teaching that concerns itself more directly with the personhood of the students, when done at all, is often pursued by a handful of individuals who may be unaware of similar efforts of any of their colleagues. Bob has accepted this constraint. He also has accepted that his peers see the needs of the students in a light different from the way he does. He carries on his work privately, concentrating on the impact he can make within the confines of his classroom.

Two of the teachers felt that their efforts regarding gender equity were strongly supported, and cited no resistance that hindered them. Both Fred and Sean felt that their support came in the form of their administration providing them substantial autonomy in most aspects of their teaching. Neither considered the broader issues of societal bias or gender bias within the structure of the school, nor whether their peers were supporting or even hindering their efforts. Instead, they confined their thoughts about the topic of support and resistance to their own activities in their individual classrooms.

Consistent with Fred's concentration on a curriculum approach of addressing gender equity, his remarks about support were directed toward access to and freedom with content and materials:

> One thing I can say about this district is they have always been real supportive about access to materials and to teaching different points of view. That's never been a problem. I think it's the same thing with the department.

Aside from a call some years ago from a parent who thought too much teaching was being directed toward "minorities," Fred has not encountered any concern from other educators, parents, or students about presenting material that incorporates gender issues.

Fred is primarily interested in equalizing interactions and providing equal gender representation within the curriculum. He has sufficient autonomy in his classroom to accomplish these things, and perhaps because he is not hampered in these efforts, he considers himself supported.

Sean extends his concept of support slightly further than does Fred. He talks of having a helpful principal, as well as having several colleagues who he believes see the world in ways similar to his view. Sean acknowledges the issue of gender bias within the school as a whole, much the way Bob does. But he dismisses the importance of systematic bias rather matter-of-factly, and concentrates on his own activities and classroom.

Here everything's very supportive. The administration is not only supportive, but encouraging. The principal is the kind of person who will say, "Is there anything we can do to make life easier?" He gets 150 percent out of everybody. As far as peers go, I think we have a pretty good mix here. I've worked with two women teachers for years, and we see things the same way. I think we have a few members here that tend to gravitate to the all-male football group, but they're very active in the school. If they want to sit together, that's fine. I generally sit at a mixed table. I just look for an empty chair.

When I taught at another middle school years ago, there were gender segregated faculty rooms. I never went to the male faculty room there. I didn't like the ethnic and gender jokes. Instead I just chose to stay in my room and work. Things are much different now, much more integrated and healthier.

During his thirty-one years of teaching, Sean has been involved in various equity movements, such as the civil rights and women's movements. Because he has long had a commitment to issues of equity, he is sensitive to incorporating whatever he can into his teaching in order to address the needs of cultural and gender groups. However, as long as he has the freedom to work with aspects of these issues in his own classes, he is not concerned about addressing gender bias beyond his classroom.

Of the eight teachers, Pam was the least concerned about the issue of support and resistance. Perhaps because she still is a long way from developing her own understanding of the place of gender equity in her teaching, she gave the question little consideration.

I don't feel I get any support, but then I don't feel I need any. There are some teachers here who are concerned about gender equity, but I don't talk to them about it. As far as resistance is concerned, I guess I don't get any.

Because Pam only does a small bit of intervention in order to counter gender bias, mostly in the form of the content she chooses to teach in her health class, she is unlikely to encounter much resistance from anyone, other than the occasional student who complains that the topic is irrelevant for her or his gender. Her failure to connect with the other teachers on her campus who she knows are interested in furthering gender equity also is symptomatic of her failure to think through ways she could more actively integrate gender equity into her teaching. Interacting with colleagues who share a commitment and interest is a powerful way to establish support for teachers who carry out work in their classrooms that might not be part of the culture of the school. Pam is ignoring an avenue that could better help her understand where and how gender equity fits into her teaching.

As each of the teachers interprets and practices gender equity in his or her classroom in an individual fashion, each perceives issues of resistance and support somewhat differently from the others. Their concerns spanned the levels within society that have been found to perpetuate gender bias: societal and parental messages to children that reinforce gender role stereotypes; the structures of schools that remain gender biased; and practices of administrators and colleagues whose behavior models, rather than counters, gender stereotypes.

Some of the teachers are satisfied, or perhaps resigned, to focus their work in gender equity within the confines of their own classrooms rather than consider any larger implications of their work. Within the fairly isolated role of teacher, they work to have an impact on their students during the time in which the students are in their classrooms. They perceive the issues of societal and school structure bias as looming too large for one teacher to change. While Mary, Sean, Fred, and Bob acknowledge the pervasive nature of gender bias outside of their classrooms, they have chosen to confine their gender equity work to that area over which they feel they have sufficient control: their own teaching.

Judy, Karen, and Beth see themselves in a larger role as catalysts for change. They speak of influencing the gender-related attitudes and behaviors of their students, the parents, their colleagues, and their supervisors. Judy works subtly and in small ways to change parents who appear to be reinforcing gender stereotypes in their children. Karen also works in modest ways on a scale greater than her classroom. She continues to remind her colleagues of their original commitment to gender equity as a foundation of the school through attention to their use of non-biased materials and language. Beth's efforts are on the largest scale. She develops programs for the female students of the school that are designed to counter societal and cultural gender bias, connects with like-minded colleagues, and is not hesitant to draw attention to gender bias present in the school.

GETTING STARTED

Having considered the information provided by the eight teachers profiled, it probably is clear to you that there is no straightforward, step-by-step means of integrating gender equity into your teaching. The variation among the teachers; their fundamental interpretations of gender equity, and their choices of which aspects of gender equity to implement into their teaching suggests that individual teachers consider and implement gender equity in fairly unique ways. There are, however, several steps that gender equity novices should take before determining their own paths.

The principle consideration is to assess your value system with regard to the issue of gender equity and your role as a teacher. Within which of the frameworks does this concept reside according to your interpretation? Do you believe that, in your position as a teacher and as someone who is committed to promoting gender equity, your focus should be on the process? In this case, you will construct your classroom in such a way that students, regardless of their gender, receive an equal distribution of resources. You will implement gender equity according to a framework of equality.

Do you believe instead that girls as a group in most situations, and boys as a group in fewer situations, are systematically disadvantaged and, as a result, require more resources than the other group? In this case, your interpretation of gender equity fits within the equitable framework. You will work to compensate for the disadvantages of those in the at-risk group, and you will allocate a greater, unequal amount of resources to them.

Or does Karen's construction of gender equity fit best with your own? Her fundamental belief about gender equity is that traditional gender stereotypes severely limit the potential of students, and that the stereotypes affecting females have provided greater limitations than those affecting males. To that extent, she views gender equity through the an equitable lens. However, in her everyday teaching, she tends to implement gender equity through the framework of equality, providing equal resources to all students while monitoring for behavior that reflects their adherence to traditional gender role stereotypes. Your determination of how you view the issue as a whole is an essential first step in thinking through how to construct a classroom that addresses gender equity.

A second early step in this process is that of assessing the culture of your school. Nearly all teachers will tell you that their schools have aspects that make them unique. There are traditions, unwritten expectations, and values that contribute to the culture of a particular site. Some schools have cultures that are more conducive to work with issues such as gender equity than others. Further, some teachers hold positions that are reasonably autonomous, and they feel free to forge ahead in their own pursuits, sometimes in conflict with the prevailing culture of the school.

As some of the teachers profiled talked about their perceptions of support and resistance in their work with gender equity, they provided insights into parts of the culture of their schools. For example, Judy talks about her supervisor, a former beauty queen, who fails to understand, and therefore to value, the issue of gender equity. However, even though Judy lacks support from her immediate supervisor, the power of her position as director of the preschool allows her to construct the environment according to her own specifications. Karen bemoans the flagging interest of her colleagues in gender equity. On the other hand, the entire school operates on the assumption that work with equity issues is of primary consideration. The structure of the school philosophy supports Karen's independent work with gender issues. Frank and Bob are pleased to be unconstrained, although not directly supported, in order to implement gender equity as they see fit. As is the case in many secondary schools, these two teachers work in considerable isolation and have some freedom to shape their classrooms according to their own views of what is best. Your school's culture and your degree of autonomy in the school should be taken into consideration. While neither of these issues need to dictate your fundamental interpretation of gender equity, they represent real-life considerations and may enhance or constrain the extent to which you realize your gender-equity goals.

Finally, while none of the profiled teachers had a particular step-by-step process that they used or that they would recommend to others, each had advice and encouragement to offer others who want to begin to integrate gender equity into their teaching. Their advice reflected several categories: self-awareness, learning the literature, and perhaps most importantly, engaging in teaching practice that is thoughtful and reflective.

In order to begin to develop a personal understanding of gender issues, the teacher must first become aware of her or his own gender biases. The term *consciousness-raising* may be appropriate here. One may choose to reflect on personal experiences of the past or the present, but some sort of personal reflection is essential. As Mary states:

> First you have to look at yourself and figure out what your own biased practices are. Only then can you consider what you are going to do in the classroom.

A number of the teachers suggested it would be helpful to find a gender-equity mentor. Teachers who share a commitment to gender equity in teaching can be helpful in monitoring exactly what is happening in your classroom with regard to gender issues. Specific teacher behaviors, such as who the teacher is calling on and who he or she is disciplining, are more objectively seen through someone else's eyes. When your teaching actions are objectively documented, you can more easily plan how to change patterns that represent gender bias.

While gender issues may be treated briefly at best in teacher training, teacher evaluation, and staff development, a great deal of literature exists about all aspects of gender bias both in schools and the larger society. All of the teachers recommended that prospective and practicing teachers educate themselves about gender equity. Their suggestions ranged from reading about women's history (Mary) to taking workshops or college courses (Fred). Beth's suggestion was:

> Read, read, read. It doesn't matter where you start. And once you start, you'll want to know more, and it will become part of you.

The last point, teaching in a reflective manner, is good advice regardless of the framework or issues being considered. But it is essential when working toward a reduction of gender bias in your teaching. Because of the complexity of sorting out your own biases as well as coming to grips with the impact of our society's messages regarding gender role expectations, it is especially important to consciously consider gender issues when teaching. Beth, within the equitable framework, believes that the process of learning to integrate gender equity into teaching is one of overcoming our own early, subtle, and profound shaping, which has had the effect of obliterating the issues of gender bias.

> As teachers, we can't do anything spontaneously. We have to make our teaching conscious behavior. I believe that there is still

so much gender bias everywhere in society, and we are all still relearning so much. So teaching in a way that is gender equitable doesn't come naturally to anyone. We have to learn how to do it, and stay on top of it forever, if we're going to make any changes.

Lastly, Karen's advice may be the most pragmatic and easiest to implement:

Just jump in. Don't be daunted. Once your consciousness is raised, it's easy to get at it, and you won't forget it because it will become part of your life. Working with gender equity doesn't take all that much, but it does entail a shift in attitude for most people. But once the point is reached where you say, "I'll work on this," the next leap is easier.

APPENDIX

INTERVIEW PROTOCOLS

Primary Interview

This interview, which was taped, then transcribed into hard copy, lasted between 1 and $2^1/_2$ hours. Each of the teachers was asked the same questions and in the same order. The questions on the interview protocol were generated from overriding concerns about gender equity issues presented by the literature.

1. Remembering back to your own school experiences, what do you recall about how girls and boys were treated?

   Do you remember anything particularly positive or negative that happened to you or others due to being a girl or boy?

   Do you think any of these experiences shaped the way you teach today?

2. In your own teacher preparation, did you have any training in gender equity?

   Tell me about it.

3. Tell me about how you plan your lessons in terms of creating gender equity, if you do that.

4. Consider this scenario: On the playground (or playing field) a group of boys are going to play a ball game. Several girls want to play, but are told by the boys that they cannot. Do you intervene? If so, how?

   If not, do you think it's ever helpful for girls and boys to have separate play activities?

5. Do you think you work with one gender of student more often than the other?

   (If so), why do you think you do that?

6. In thinking about the students in your class(es), can you identify the leaders?

   Are they more likely to be boys or girls?

   Why do you think those students are leaders?

7. Does it seem to you that girls or boys in your class(es) talk more, or in general dominate the class?

   (If so), why do you think this happens?

8. Do boys or girls seem to be more of a discipline or behavioral problem in your classroom?

   Why do you think this is so?

9. When you consider gender equity in your classes, how do you use materials to help you make your points or meet your goals?

10. Are you ever aware that some teaching methods might be more effective for males or females?

    Tell me about that.

11. Do you intentionally seat or otherwise group your students in order to meet any gender equity goals?

    (If so), how do you do that?

12. Describe how your students react to any materials/activities you use that deal with gender equity.

13. What do you look for in materials, and how do you select your materials?

14. How do you use these materials?

15. Describe the type of support you feel you get from your colleagues and/or administrators in your work with gender equity.

    Describe any resistance.

16. Is there anything you feel we have not discussed that is important to your ideas about gender equity in your teaching?

Contact Summary Form

The contact summary form was used for each classroom observation. The general categories used to structure the observations were derived from the literature and represent dominant themes in gender equity teaching.

1. What did I notice about the lesson, content, or curriculum by gender?
   Whose work (by gender) is noticeable in the class?
   What subjects were taught?
   Who is in the class by gender?

2. Teacher: Student interactions
   QUANTITY?
   Frequency of contact by gender?
   Describe the verbal contact.
   Describe the non-verbal contacts.
   Who does the teacher touch?
   QUALITY?
   Who is disciplined and how?
   Who is praised and how?

3. Student: Student interactions
   Student conversations: Who talks the most?
   What do they talk about?
   Who does not talk at all?
   Who are the leaders and what makes me think this?

4. Methods
   What instructional methods does the teacher use?
   What is the organization of the classroom? Does this seem to facilitate gender equity or hinder it?
   What words does the teacher use during instruction or other interaction? Are the words gender-neutral or biased?
   Who does the teacher monitor? How?

5. Diagram of the classroom, including furniture and people. Designate where the action zone is located.

6. What were the main issues that struck me during this visit?

REFERENCES

CHAPTER 1. INTRODUCING GENDER EQUITY

Csikszentmihaly, M. (1988), *Optimal Experience* (New York: Cambridge University Press).

Freeman, D. (1983), *Margaret Mead and Samoa: The Making and Unmaking of an Anthropological Myth* (Cambridge, Mass.: Harvard University Press).

Grayson, D.A. & Martin, M.D. (1988), *Gender/Ethnic Expectations and Student Achievement* (Earlham, Iowa: GrayMill).

Hyde, J. S. & Linn, M. C. (1986), eds. *The Psychology of Gender: Advances through Meta-analysis* (Baltimore: The Johns Hopkins University Press).

Mead, M. (1935), *Sex and Temperament in Three Primitive Societies* (New York: New American Library).

Muuse, R. E. (1988), *Theories of Adolescence* (New York: Random House).

National Advisory Council on Women's Educational Progress, U.S. Department of Education, *Title IX: The Half Full, Half Empty Glass* (Washington, D.C.: U.S. Government Printing Office).

New Pioneers Seminar Leader's Handbook (1975), Women's Educational Equity Act Program (U.S. Department of Health, Education, and Welfare, Office of Education).

Richmond-Abbott, M. (1983), *Sex Roles over the Life Cycle* (New York: McGraw-Hill).

Sadker, M.; Sadker, D.; & Klein, S. (1991), The issue of gender in elementary and secondary education. In G. Grant, ed. *Review of Research in Education*, 17 (Washington, D.C.: American Educational Research Association).

Secada. W. G., ed. (1989), *Equity in Education* (New York: Falmer Press).

Tittle, C. K. (1985), Assumptions about the nature and value of sex equity. In S. Klein, ed. *Handbook for Achieving Sex Equity through Education*, 13–15 (Baltimore: The Johns Hopkins University Press).

Webster's New Collegiate Dictionary (1975) (G. & C. Merriam Co.: Springfield, Mass.).

CHAPTER 2. SOCIALIZATION

Bem, S. (1975), Sex-role adaptability: One consequence of psychological androgyny. *Journal of Personality and Social Psychology,* 31:634–643.

Callahan, R. (1967), *Education and the Cult of Efficiency,* University of Chicago Press: Chicago. In Stockard, J., et al. (1980), *Sex Equity in Education* (New York: Academic Press).

Carelli, A. O. (1988), *Sex Equity in Education* (Springfield, Ill.: Charles C. Thomas).

Cherry, L. (1975), The preschool teacher-child dyad: Sex differences in verbal interaction. *Child Development,* 46:532–535. In G. Grant, ed. *Review of Research in Education* (Washington, D.C.: American Educational Research Association).

Clabaugh, G. K. & Razycki, E. G. (1990), *Understanding Schools: Foundations of Education* (New York: Harper & Row).

Coleman, J. (1960), Athletics in high school. In David, D. S. & Brannon, R. (1976), eds. *The Forty-Nine Percent Majority: The Male Sex Role* (Reading, Mass.: Addison-Wesley).

Comstock, G. & Paik, H. (1991), *Television and the American Child* (San Diego: Academy Press).

Conley. S. (1991). Review of research on teacher participation in school decision making. In G. Grant, ed. *Review of Research in Education* (Washington, D.C.: American Educational Research Association).

Fagot, B. (1978), The influence of sex of child on parental reactions to toddler children. *Child Development,* 49:462.

Fennema, E. & Meyer, M. R. (1989). In W. G. Secada, ed. *Equity in Education* (New York: Falmer Press).

Frueh, T. & McGhee, P. E. (1975), Traditional sex-role development and amount of time spent watching television. *Sunday Times,* 12 August, p. 35.

Goodsell, W. (1931), *Pioneers of Women's Education in the United States* (New York: AMS Press).

Hammer, C. & Gerald, E. (1990), *Selected Characteristics of Public and Private School Administrators (Principals): 1987–88* (Washington, D.C.: National Center for Education Statistics, Office of Educational Research and Improvement, U.S. Department of Education).

Hill, C. (1967), *Society and Puritanism in Pre-revolutionary England* (New York: Schocken).

Hoffman, N. (1981), *Women's True Profession: Voices from the History of Teaching* (Old Westbury, N.Y.: Feminist Press).

Kessler-Harris, A. (1989), Women, work, and the social order. In L. Richardson & V. Taylor, eds. *Feminist Frontiers II: Rethinking Sex, Gender, and Society* (New York: McGraw Hill).

Knight, E. W. (1941), *Education in the United States* (New York: Ginn).

Larkin, J. (1988), *The Reshaping of Everyday Life* (New York: Harper & Row).

McGhee, P. E. & Frueh, T. (1980), Television viewing and the learning of sex-role sterotypes. *Sex Roles*, 6:179–188.

Maccoby, E. (1971), *The Development of Sex Differences* (Stanford, Calif.: Stanford University Press).

Maccoby, E. & Jacklin, C. (1974), *The Psychology of Sex Differences* (Stanford, Calif.: Stanford University Press).

Monroe, P., ed. (1913), *A Cyclopedia of Education* (New York: Macmillian).

Richardson, L. & Taylor, C. (1989), Feminist Frontiers II: Rethinking Sex, Gender, and Society (New York: McGraw-Hill).

Richmond-Abbott, M. (1983), *Masculine and Feminine: Sex Roles over the Life Cycle* (New York: McGraw-Hill).

Rosaldo, M. (1980), The use and abuse of anthropology: Reflections on feminism and cross-cultural understanding. *Signs*, 5(3):389–417.

Rubin, J.; Provenzano, F.; & Luria, Z. (1974), The eye of the beholder: Parents' views of sex of newborns. *American Journal of Orthopsychiatry*, 44:512–519.

Ruble, D.; Balaban, T.; & Cooper, J. (1981), Gender constancy and the effects of sex-typed television toy commericals. *Child Development*, 52:667–673.

Sadker, M. P. & Sadker, D. M. (1982), *Sex Equity Handbook for Schools* (Longman: New York).

Sadker, M.; Sadker, D.; & Klein, S. (1991), The issue of gender in elementary and secondary education. In G. Grant, ed. *Review of Research in Education* (Washington, D.C.: American Educational Research Association).

Sanday, P. (1981), *Female Power and Male Dominance* (Cambridge: Cambridge University Press).

Sanger, W. (1958), *A History of Prostitution* (New York: Harper), quoted in Bullough, V. (1974), *The Subordinate Sex* (Baltimore: Penquin Books), p. 11.

Schmuck, P. (1980), Differentiation by sex in educational professions. In J. Stockard, P. Schmuck, K. Kempner, P. Williams, S. K. Edson, & M. A. Smith (1980), *Sex Equity in Education* (New York: Academic Press).

Serbin, L. A.; O'Leary, K. D.; Kent, R. N.; & Tonick, I. J. (1973), A comparison of teacher response to the preacademic and problem behavior of boys and girls. *Child Development*, 44:796–804.

Serbin, L. A. & O'Leary, K. D. (1975), How nursery schools teach girls to shut up. *Psychology Today*, July, 56–58, 102–103.

Smith, C. & Lloyd, B. (1978), Maternal behavior and perceived sex of infant: Revisited. *Child Development*, 49:1263–1265.

Stevens, E. & Woods, G. H. (1987), *Justice, Ideology, and Education* (New York: Random House).

Stock, P. (1978), *Better than Rubies: A History of Women's Education* (New York: G. P. Putnam's Sons).

Stockard, J.; Schmuck. P. A.; Kempner, K.; Williams, P.; Edson, S. K.; & Smith, M. A. (1980), *Sex Equity in Education* (New York: Academic Press).

Tanner, N. & Zhilman, A. (1976), Women in evolution: Innovation and selection in human origins. In M. Richmond-Abbott (1983), *Masculine and Feminine: Sex Roles over the Life Cycle* (New York: McGraw-Hill).

Thorne, B. (1986), Girls and boys together . . . but mostly apart: Gender arrangements in elementary schools. In W. W. Hartup & Z. Rubin, eds. *Relationships and Development* (Hillsdale, N.J.: Lawrence Erlbaum Associates).

Tuchman, G. (1978), The symbolic annihilation of women by the mass media. In G. Tuchman, A. K. Daniels, & J. Genet, eds. *Images of Women in the Mass Media* (New York: Oxford University Press).

Vaerting, M. & Vaerting, M. (1923), *The Dominant Sex: A Study in the Sociology of Sex Differentiation* (New York: Doran). In Bullough, V. (1974), *The Subordinate Sex* (Baltimore: Penguin Books).

Weiler, K. (1989), Women's history and the history of women teachers. *Journal of Education,* 171 (3):9–31.

Women and Minorities in School Administration: Facts and Figures (1988–90). American Association of School Administrators.

Women on Words and Images (1975), *Channeling Children: Sex Stereotyping on Primetime TV* (Princeton, N.J.: Princeton University Press).

Woody, T. (1929), *A History of Women's Education in the United States* (Lancaster, Penn.: Science Press). In K. Weiler (1989). Women's history and the history of women teachers. *Journal of Education,* 171(3):9–31.

Zeigler, H. & Tucker, H. (1979), Final report on the responsiveness of public schools to their clientele (University of Oregon).

Zucherman, S. (1979), In D. Haraway, Animal sociology and a natural economy of the body politic. *Signs,* 4:37–60.

CHAPTER 3. CURRICULUM

Aiken, L. (1971), Intellective variables and mathematics achievement: Directions for research. *Journal of School Psychology,* 9:201.

Aiken, L. (1970), Attitudes toward mathematics. *Review of Educational Research,* 40:551–596.

Bottomley, J. & Ormerod, M. (1981), Stability and ability in science interest from middle school to the age of science choices. (14). *European Journal of Science Education,* 3(3):329–338.

Campbell, P. & Metz, S. (1987), What does it take to increase the number of women majoring in engineering? Conference proceedings of the American Society for Engineering Education, 882–887. In the AAUW Report (1992), How Schools Shortchange Girls. The AAUW Educational Foundation.

Carelli, A. O. (1988), ed. *Sex Equity in Education: Readings and Strategies* (Springfield, Ill.: Thomas).

Clark, C. O. (1972), A determination of commonalities of science interests held by intermediate grade children in inner-city, suburban, and rural schools. *Science Education,* 65(2):125–136.

Curran, L. (1980), Science education: Did she drop out or was she pushed? In L. Birke, ed. *Alice Through the Microscope* (London: Virago).

DeBoer, G. E. (1984), A study of gender effects in the science and mathematics course-taking behavior of a group of students who graduated from college in the late 1970s. *Journal of Research in Science Teaching,* 21(1):95–105.

Erickson, G. L. & Erickson, L. J. (1984), Females and science achievement: Evidence, explanations and implication. *Science Education,* 68(2):63–89.

Ernest, J. (1976), *Mathematics and Sex* (Santa Barbara: University of California, Department of Mathematics).

Fennema, E. (1985), Success in Mathematics. In Marland, M., ed. *Sex Differentiation and Schooling* (London: Heinemann Educational Books).

Fennema, E.; Peterson, P., Carpenter, T. P., & Lubinski, C. A. (1990), Teachers' attributions and beliefs about girls, boys, and mathematics. *Educational Studies in Mathematics,* 21:55–69.

Fennema, E. & Meyer, M. R. (1989), Gender, equity, and mathematics. In Secada, W. G., ed. *Equity in Education* (New York: Falmer Press).

Fennema, E. & Sherman, J. (1977), Sex-related differences in mathematics achievement, spatial visualization, and affective factors. *American Educational Research Journal,* 14:51–71.

Fennema, E. & Sherman, J. (1978), Sex-related differences in mathematics achievement and related factors: A further study. *Journal for Research in Mathematics Education,* 9:189–203.

Fox, L. H.; Brody, L.; & Tobin, D., eds. (1980), *Women and the Mathematical Mystique* (Baltimore: Johns Hopkins University Press).

Friedman, L. (1989), Mathematics and the gender gap: A meta-analysis of recent studies on sex differences in mathematical tasks. *Review of Educational Research,* 59:185–213.

Hulme, M. A. (1988), Mirror, mirror on the wall: Biased reflections in textbooks and instructional materials. In Carelli, A. O., ed. *Sex Equity in Education: Readings and Strategies* (Springfield, Ill.: Thomas).

Hyde, J. S. & Linn, M. C. (1986), eds. *The Psychology of Gender: Advances through Meta-Analysis* (Baltimore: Johns Hopkins University Press).

Klein, S. S. (1985), ed. *Handbook for Achieving Sex Equity through Education* (Baltimore: Johns Hopkins University Press).

Maccoby, E. E. & Jacklin, C. N. (1974), *The Psychology of Sex Differences* (Stanford, Calif.: Stanford University Press).

McLeod, J. & Silverman, S. (1973), *You Won't Do: What Textbooks on U. S. Government Teach High School Girls* (Pittsburgh, Penn.: KNOW).

Parsons, J. E.; Adler, T. F.; & Kaczala, C. (1982), Socialization of achievement attitudes and beliefs: Parental influences. *Child Development*, 53:310–321.

Parsons, J. E.; Kaczala, C.; & Meece, J. (1982), Socialization of achievement attitudes and beliefs: Classroom influences. *Child Development*, 53:322–339.

Reyes, L. H. & Padilla, M. J. (1985), Science, math, and gender. *The Science Teacher*, 52:46–48.

Reyes, L. H. & Stanic, G. (1988), Race, sex, and math. *Journal of Research in Math Education*, 19:26–43.

Richmond-Abbott, M. (1983), *Masculine and Feminine: Sex Roles over the Life Cycle* (New York: McGraw-Hill).

Sadker, M. P. & Sadker, D. M. (1982), *Sex Equity Handbook for Schools* (New York: Longman).

Scott, K. P.; Dwyer, C. A.; & Lieb-Brilhart, B. (1985), Sex equity in reading and communication skills. in Klein, S. S., ed. *Handbook for Achieving Sex Equity through Education* (Baltimore: Johns Hopkins University Press).

Scott, K. P. & Schau, C. G. (1985), Sex equity and sex bias in instructional materials. In Klein, S. S., ed. *Handbook for Achieving Sex Equity through Education* (Baltimore: Johns Hopkins University Press).

Sherman, J. (1980), Mathematics, spatial visualization, and related factors: Changes in girls and boys, grades 8–11. *Journal of Educational Psychology*, 72:476–482.

Sherman, J. & Fennema, E. (1977), The study of mathematics by high school girls and boys: Related variables. *American Educational Research Journal*, 14:159–168.

Sudan, M. N. & Riedesel, C. A. (1969), *Interpretive Study of Research and Development in Elementary School Mathematics*. Vol. 1. Final Report, project no. 8–0586 (U.S. Department of Health, Education, and Welfare).

Thompson, S. K. (1975), Gender labels and early sex-role development. *Child Development,* 46:339–347.

Tobias, S. (1978), *Overcoming Math Anxiety* (New York: Norton).

U.S. Department of Education, Office of Educational Research and Improvement, National Center for Education Statistics. Digest of Education Statistics (1990).

Weitzman, L. & Rizzo, D. (1976), *Biased Textbooks* and *Images of Males and Females in Elementary School Textbooks* (Washington, D.C.: Resource Center on Sex Roles in Education).

Winfield, L. & Lee, V. (1986), Gender differences in reading proficiency: Are they constant across racial groups? In the AAUW Report (1992), How schools shortchange girls (The AAUW Educational Foundation).

Women on Words and Images. (1975), *Dick and Jane as Victims: Sex Stereotyping in Children's Readers, Help Wanted: Sexism in Career Education Materials* (Princeton, N.J.: Princeton University Press).

CHAPTER 4. TEACHING METHODS

Adams, R. S. & Biddle, B. J. (1970), *Realities of Teaching: Explorations with Videotape* (New York: Holt, Rinehart and Winston).

Allport, G. (1954), *The Nature of Prejudice* (Cambridge, Mass.: Addison-Wesley).

Arends, R. I. (1988), *Learning to Teach* (New York: Random House).

Block, J. H. (1984), *Sex Role Identity and Ego Development* (San Francisco: Jossey-Bass).

Bossert, S. T. (1981), Understanding sex differences in children's classroom experiences. *The Elementary Journal,* 81(5):356–74.

Clement, D. & Eisenhart, M. (1979), *Learning Gender Roles in a Southern Elementary School: Final Report* (Chapel Hill, N.C.: Spencer Foundation).

DeStanfo, J. S. (1976), *Personal Communication* (Columbus: Ohio State University).

Dewey, J. (1916), *Democracy and Education* (New York: Macmillan).

Fox, L. S. (1977). The effects of sex role socialization on mathematics participation and achievement. In Fox, L., Fennema, E., & Sherman, J., *Women and Mathematics: Research Perspectives for Change* (NIE Papers in Education and Work, No. 8 (Washington, D.C.: National Institute of Education).

Fox, L. H. (1976), Sex differences in mathematical precocity: Bridging the gap. In D. F. Keating, ed. *Intellectual Talent: Research and Development* (Baltimore: Johns Hopkins University Press).

Grayson, D. A. & Martin, M. D. (1985), Gender expectations and student achievement. Los Angeles County Office of Education. Division of Project Funding and Management.

Johnson, D. W. & Johnson, R. T. (1975), *Learning Together and Alone: Cooperation, Competition, and Individualization* (Englewood Cliffs, N.J.: Prentice-Hall).

Kramarea, C. (1975). Woman's speech: Separate but unequal? In B. Thorne & N. Henley, eds. *Language and Sex: Difference and Dominance* (Rowley, Mass.: Newbury House).

Lockheed, M. E. (1981), *Year One Report: Classroom Interaction, Student Cooperation, and Leadership* (Princeton, N.J.: Educational Testing Service).

MacKay, D. G. (1983), Prescriptive grammar and the pronoun problem. In B. Thorne, C. Kramarae, & N. Henley, eds. *Language, Gender, and Society* (Rowley, Mass.: Newbury House).

Richardson, L. (1989), Gender stereotyping in the English language. In Richardson, L. & Taylor, V., eds. *Feminist Frontiers II: Rethinking Sex, Gender, and Society* (New York: McGraw-Hill).

Sadker, M. P. & Sadker, D. M. (1982), *Sex Equity Handbook for Schools* (New York: Longman).

Slavin, R.; Sharon, S.; Kagan, S.; Hertz-Lazarowitz, R.; Webb, C.; & Schmuck, R., eds. (1985), *Learning to Cooperate, Cooperating to Learn* (New York: Plenum Press).

Slavin, R. (1983), *Cooperative Learning* (New York: Longman).

Stanley, J. P. (1977), Pragmatic woman: The prostitute. In D. L. Shores, ed. *Papers in Language Variation* (Birmingham: University of Alabama Press).

Webster's New Collegiate Dictionary (1975) (Springfield, Mass.: G. & C. Merriam).

Wilkinson-Cherry, L. & Subkoviak, M. (1982). In Grayson, D. A. & Martin, M. D. (1985), Gender Expectations and Student Achievement. Los Angeles County Office of Education, Division of Project Funding and Management.

CHAPTER 5. TEACHER INTERACTIONS

Dweck, C. S.; Davidson, W.; Nelson, S.; & Enna, B. (1978). Sex differences in learned helplessness: II, The contingencies of evaluative feedback in the classroom and III, An experimental analysis. *Developmental Psychology*, 14:268–278.

Dweck, C. & Gilliard, D. (1975, Expectancy statements as determinants of reactions to failure: Sex differences in persistence and expectancy change. *Journal of Personality and Social Psychology*, 32:1077–1084.

Ebbeck, M. (1984). Equity for boys and girls: Some important issues. *Early Child Development and Care*, 18:119–131.

Fennema, E. & Peterson, P. (1987), Effective Teaching for Girls and Boys: The Same or Different? In *Talks to Teachers*. D. Berliner and B. Rosenshine, eds. (New York: Random House), 111–125.

Good, R.; Sikes, J. N.; & Brophy, J. E. (1973), Effects of teacher sex on classroom interaction. *Journal of Educational Psychology,* 65(1): 74–87.

Irvine, J. J. (1986), Teacher-student interactions: Effects of: Student race, sex, and grade level. *Journal of Educational Psychology,* 78(1):14–21.

Irvine, J. J. (1985), Teacher communication patterns as related to the race and sex of the student. *Journal of Educational Research,* 78(6):338–345.

Meyer, W. J. & Thompson, G. G. (1956), Sex differences in the distribution of teacher approval and disapproval among sixth-grade children. *Journal of Educational Psychology,* 47:385–397.

Putnam, S. E. & Self, P. A. (1988), Social Play in Toddlers: Teacher Intrusions (ED 319 529).

Serbin, L. A.; O'Leary, K. D.; Kent, R. N.; & Tonic, I. J. (1973), A comparison of teacher response to the pre-academic and problem behavior of boys and girls. *Child Development,* 44(4):796–804.

Simpson, A. W. & Erickson, M. T. (1983), Teachers' verbal and nonverbal communication patterns as a function of teacher race, student gender, and student race. *American Educational Research Journal,* 20(2):183–198.

CHAPTER 6. TOWARD GENDER EQUITY IN YOUR CLASSROOM

The AAUW Report: How Schools Shortchange Girls (1992). The AAUW Educational Foundation, Wellesley College Center for Research on Women.

Carelli, A. O. (1988), *Sex Equity in Education* (Springfield, Ill.: Charles C. Thomas).

Dewey, J. (1916), *Democracy and Education* (New York: Macmillan).

Digest of Education Statistics (1989) (1990) Department of Education, Office of Educational Research and Improvement, National Center for Education Statistics (NCES 91–660).

Good, R.; Sikes, J. N.; & Brophy, J. E. (1973), Effects of teacher sex on classroom interaction. *Journal of Educational Psychology,* 65(1): 74–87.

Hill, C. (1967), *Society and Puritanism in Pre-revolutionary England* (New York: Schocken).

Richmond-Abbott, M. (1983), *Masculine and Feminine: Sex Roles over the Life Cycle* (New York: McGraw-Hill).

Rubin, J.; Provanzano, F.; & Luria, Z. (1974), The eye of the beholder: Parents' views of sex of newborns. *American Journal of Orthopsychiatry*, 44:512–519.

Sadker, M. P. & Sadker, D. M. (1982), *Sex Equity Handbook for Schools* (New York: Longman).

Scott, K. P.; Dwyer, C. A.; & Lieb-Brilhart, B. (1985), Sex equity in reading and communication skills. In Klein, S. S. ed., *Handbook for Achieving Sex Equity through Education* (Baltimore: Johns Hopkins University Press).

Secada, W., ed. (1989), *Sex Roles over the Life Cycle* (New York: McGraw-Hill).

Serbin, L. A.; O'Leary, K. D.; Kent, R. M.; & Tonic, I. J. (1973), A comparison of teacher response to the pre-academic and problem behavior of boys and girls. *Child Development* 44(4):796–804.

Slavin, R.; Sharon, S.; Kagan, S.; Hertz-Lazarowitz, R.; Webb, C.; & Schmuck, R., eds. (1985), *Learning to Cooperate, Cooperating to Learn* (New York: Plenum Press).

Slavin, R. (1983), *Cooperative Learning* (New York: Longman).

INDEX